Saint Antonino
and
Mediæval Economics

Saint Antonino
and
Mediæval Economics

Bede Jarrett, O.P.

XIII Books
An Imprint of Arouca Press
PO Box 55003
Bridgeport PO
Waterloo, ON N2J 0A5
Canada
www.aroucapress.com
Send inquiries to info@aroucapress.com

Originally published by B. Herder (St. Louis) &
Manresa Press (London) in 1914.

ISBN: 978-1-998492-57-2

Contents

Introduction

THE chief justification that can be urged for this Life of Saint Antonino is to be derived from the value of his economic theories. These are so eminently reasonable and yet so flamingly ideal, so soberly described by him and yet so sincerely Christian, that they must make their appeal to every reader. We are so often repeating that we live in a time of crisis, that civilization stands at the crossways, that the outlook towards the future promises few prospects of hope; we are so increasingly struck by the difficulties that loom ahead of us, so terrified even by the signs of the times, that it is surely good for us to watch how another, in a period of stress and trouble, rose to the height of his great position and brought an answer to the questionings of his own generation.

For the times were certainly troublous all over Europe when S. Antonino was passing through his boyhood. In religion he found that Christendom was itself driven asunder over the succession to the Papacy. Two, and later three, claimants disputed the throne of the Fisherman. This seemed to so many at that time, who were filled with deep reverence for the Bride of Christ, as the hardest trial to Faith. What did the ravage of the Plague matter, or the relaxation of the bonds of religious life, compared with this seeming failure of that power, which, in their eyes, alone could have restored everything in Christ? The city might still be set upon its hill, yet what did that advantage the people of God if a thick mist of clouds had drifted round its pinnacles and towers?

The spirit, too, of lawlessness and revolt was abroad all over the West. In England, the rising of the Peasantry, which we commonly associate with Wat Tyler and John Ball, "the mad priest of Kent," had been at one time sufficiently serious to make the stability of the Crown itself seem for the moment in imminent peril; indeed, only the courage of the boy King and the lying promise of instant reform broke up perhaps the most formidable rebellion that has ever threatened this country. Nor was this Peasant Revolt an isolated occurrence, but it was rather symptomatic of a European movement, which some indeed have attempted to explain by suggesting that it was supported by a definite organization, international and anti-social. The next year saw a similar disturbance in Florence. The *Ciompi*, or disfranchised masses, tired of their exploitation by the few freemen who managed the whole government of the city, attempted to overturn the machinery of the Republic. At the root of this trouble, as at the root of the English Revolt, was certainly an economic grievance, the scarcity of wages, the dearness of provisions, and the immemorial bondage which custom imposed upon the worker. The effect of this outbreak might have been extremely serious but for the exertions of Michel Lando, a huge wool-comber, who had been elected, under the threat of mob violence, to the supreme magistracy of Florence. He had great restraining influence over his own party, and by the exercise of his personal ascendancy—and also, it must be added, by the use of his physical strength—he succeeded in moderating the demands of his followers and preventing any wanton destruction or even much disorder at all.

A third revolt which, in its synchronism, again suggests some definite connection between France and the labour-leaders in England and Italy, was the rising of the *Maillotins* of Paris. In 1382, the reimposition of taxes, which the King had promised to remit, passed the limit of popular patience, and the people barricaded the streets and overawed the Government. The obnoxious taxes were repealed, a complete amnesty promised to all the rebels, and the civic privileges and charters confirmed. But, as in the case of the English rising, the terms given by the Government were never observed. So long as the mob was strong enough to defend its own interests, it could live in impunity. It even offered a large sum of money to the Crown in gratitude for its favours. But the moment that an army strong in repute, after a decisive victory over the Flemings, approached the city, the royal officials tore up their treaties, broke the oaths even of amnesty, and after punishing the leaders of the revolt with the extreme rigour of the law, refused to acknowledge the liberties granted to the city. The spirit of revolt had been met in every case by the superiority of physical force and by a cynical disregard for all agreements made under the stress of popular agitation.

It is curious to note that this series of revolts by the people was followed by a series of depositions of ruling sovereigns by their subjects and by a corresponding series of civil wars. The deposition of Richard II of England at the hands of the House of Lancaster, as Shakespeare has cleverly shown in his historical plays, led to the Wars of the Roses, which, however, were delayed by the success of Henry V in draining all military forces out of the Kingdom by engaging them in a war with France. That campaign of Agincourt gave the House of Lancaster a respite, which, however, the youth and weakness of Henry VI prevented from being of much avail.

But in Germany, civil war followed almost immediately on the deposition of Wenzel, King of the Romans. His cousin, Jost, the evil genius of the House of Luxembourg, attempted to secure for himself the vacant dignity but found that Wenzel's brother, Sigismund, was a serious rival for the Crown. Together they fought for its possession, and in their struggle, it nearly escaped from them altogether; but the timely and sudden death of Jost left Sigismund alone as head of the Empire.

The Church followed along the same lines of procedure, and a portion of it, by means of some recalcitrant cardinals, deposed the rival pontiffs. Deposition was one of the remedies which seemed then to have suggested itself as an easy way out of difficulties. If rulers did not fulfil their appointed duties to the satisfaction of their subjects, the most obvious method, the simplest, was to get rid of them and substitute for them others who would be likely to be more useful to the general good. This plan has always found favour with men whose ideas of redress are limited to the narrow outlook of their own generation. They forget, or perhaps do not care to remember, that the result of this is but to sow the seeds of civil war. The adherents of the deposed monarch, when his evil deeds have had time to lose their sting, point with scorn to the ill-success of the newer dynasty and have always plenty of opportunity for noticing that promises made, when the throne was as yet only in sight, have been broken when policy no longer necessitated their being kept. The simplest remedy therefore succeeds only for the time and conjures up itself far greater evils than it can allay. In the Church, in France, in Aragon and elsewhere, came a crop of civil wars, reaped after depositions.

Then with the healing of the Schism at Constance, where the rival popes resigned but were not deposed, came a note of peace. The disputes that had for long dissolved the unity of Christendom were almost immediately ended by compromise. The Hussites, at least the more

moderate party among them, made their sub-
mission on the acceptance by the Church of certain articles which satisfied their claims in the
theological dispute. Cosimo de' Medici, whose
banishment from Florence had unsettled the
balance of power, was brought back to his despotism on the award of the Pontiff. The Papacy
itself came to terms with France at Bourges
and with Germany at Mainz, while the lengthy
Schism that had for centuries split East and
West was healed at the Council of Florence in
1439.

Altogether it is apparent that just when S.
Antonino was coming into a position of power
and influence, Europe was itself settling down
after a long nightmare of plague, schism, risings,
depositions, and civil wars. Hence it is, no doubt,
that the writings of the Saint are filled with such
optimism. He is not as one without hope; rather
in his burning sense of the inherent goodness of
human nature, in his steadfast trust in the value
of clear teaching to a world ahungered for it,
his language reminds the reader of the glowing
declamation of the French Revolutionaries. It
must be admitted that apart from some definite
institutions for the poor and sick and for children, the practical effect of the Archbishop's
treatises do not seem to have been considerable.
He does not appear to have in any way changed
the course of events in matters social nor to have
converted for long the public opinion, even of his
native city, to the principles of justice. Yet it is

something to have held up to the views of men an ideal of Christian polity, of social life, of the high ethics of commerce. It is not wholly vain for the spiritual power of the world to have shown in what light it considered the problems of human destiny and the progress of the race. The people may not follow the vision, but woe to the prophet who is silent, who will not announce it to all that have ears to hear! Woe especially to the prophet who is oppressed, numbed, paralyzed by the seeming uselessness of telling his burden, and who, out of sheer weariness and cynical despair, is made dumb.

We say a prophet, for it is not to be forgotten that the Saint writes on the problems of economics only as a moralist. He does not set up to be a judge or a divider except from the point of view of moral justice. In his volumes there is no pretence of much acquaintance with the political theories of his own time, except in so far as they touched on matters where the Church's guardianship of morality required to be exercised. But it is just in this capacity that his writings are most valuable, for it is rare to find so exquisite a judgment as his, so fine and nice in its appreciation of the difficulties that beset the life of trade. Men at that time, however far short they fell of the ideal of perfect justice, still clung to the principles of the Christian Faith. Their laws were based upon the acceptance of the Church's teaching, though the administration of them was certainly not always conducted in a spirit of mercy and truth. Still the framework of society was definitely Christian, and men continuously sought to discover how to adjust the experiment of daily life to the changing circumstances of social conditions. That this was so is evident from the way in which S. Antonino was called upon by men of all classes to decide for them knotty questions, where the clear lines of justice and right were not altogether manifest. He was appealed to on every possible occasion, and his careful and prudent judgment evidently approved itself to his questioners.

It must also be remembered that at this date the position of the merchants in Europe was quite considerable. Even in England, where the baronage and feudal chiefs had a very great influence in the State, the great families were entering into trade, and the trading families were themselves taking an important place in the national affairs. The names of the de la Poles, who rose from commerce to the highest places in the State; of the Canynges, whose wealth was the mainstay of Bristol and whose magnificent Church of St. Mary, Redcliffe remains as a testimony of their splendour; of the more famous Dick Whittington, were high in public honour, and carried weight in the national councils. But in Italy the free cities and republics were essentially trading centres, and there the merchant princes, by their adventure, their wealth, their judicious patronage of the arts, took the lead in the direction of politics. Where commerce was so necessary for the existence of the city, it naturally had a preponderating voice in the conduct of affairs.

Moreover, the trade routes of the continent were also the great roadways of the world. Armies marching to battle had to pass along by the centres of manufacture and commerce. Pilgrims to the shrines of Christendom had no other means of progress except in company with the trading caravans that went up and down the world with the produce of loom, of harvest, of forest, and of the generous bounty of nature. Consequently all the movements of the world made their advance along the lines that led past the great cities, which thus became increasingly concerned in all political happenings and were therefore eager to take their share in the settlement of them. Hence at the time of S. Antonino it may almost be said that the older domination of the West by the universities, or even by the kings, had given way to the rule of trade. The sovereigns themselves based their policy on the economic needs of their subjects. Their wars were fought for commercial ends. Their counsellors were not unfrequently taken from the commercial classes. Their very armies were paid for by the contributions of traders, who, as the price of their subsidies, extorted from the Government, in return, fuller commercial privileges. Even the advance of the Turk was now resisted, not so much on the plea that Constantinople was a city sacred by the

consecration of Christian worship, but as the
great trade-door between East and West, the
last portal that remained for the entrance into
Europe of the spice trade, the precious metals,
and the elaborate wealth of the Orient. It was
trade itself that set on foot the great discoveries
by the Portuguese and Spaniards, and the con-
tinuation of these adventures depended almost
wholly on the amount of wealth that they were
supposed to bring into the countries that fitted
out the exploring fleets. We know, for example, that the rounding of the shoulder of West
Africa was delayed for many years because the
number of slaves brought home from the coast
was at first very small, insufficient to make the
expeditions pay.

In every way, therefore, commerce was taking
up a dominating place in European politics. This
S. Antonino could see as well as anyone else,
but he saw also the terrible evils such an event
was bound to bring in its train unless something were done to make the rule of the rich
follow the laws of God. S. Francis of Assisi had
made his answer to the difficulty at an earlier
stage by his chivalrous vows to "Lady Poverty."
But that high ideal was ceasing to appeal to an
age that had outgrown the poetry and charm of
such a voice. Not the ideal of renunciation, not
the *Thebaid*, but the right control of the springs
of wealth could alone save the generations that
were to follow from the disastrous effect of
this overpowering domination. The pursuit of

riches appears to contest with sport (perhaps it is itself part of the same spirit), the chief place among the interests that fascinate our human energies. Its rule, therefore, is not unlikely to banish all other considerations for the minds of men, to silence conscience, to stifle pity, to make honesty only a policy and not a moral or ethical principle. It is good policy, but something more.

To set up the standard of Justice, to lay the foundations of society on the laws of God, to make men look at economics through the eyes of Faith was the high endeavour of this great man.

Did he succeed or fail? Perhaps the reading of his theories, of his very words, may turn our thoughts to find therein the remedies that our own age still needs. Perhaps the suggestions that he makes for the ultimate settlement of all social problems by the principles of truth and justice may bear fruit in our own time. Perhaps we ourselves may help to answer the query, whether he failed or succeeded. But certainly it is, above all, essential to notice this witness to the unseen worth of things, this trumpet-call to lay up treasure in heaven. "And when the time comes, as come it will, when society as a whole recognizes that big fortunes and starvation are alike intolerable and must be put an end to, God grant it may discover at the same time that the mad rush for wealth is folly and sin, and that a life of greater leisure in which to cultivate the higher faculties of our being and the sweeter and finer sides of our total experience is infinitely to be preferred to the life of fever and tumult, and of base and sordid values, that so many of us are living now."

Chronicle of Contemporary Events to Show Unrest Gradually Quieting

I

The Night of Fore-Being

SAINT ANTONINO was a Florentine of the *Quattrocento*, a writer on social and political questions, and a canonised Dominican Archbishop. His claim, therefore, on us is threefold.

As a Florentine he entered into a splendid inheritance. The Revival of Learning, whensoever we date its beginnings, had at his birth greatly advanced in its stately course. Its early dawn had flushed all Florence with a passionate desire for the beauties of the antique world. Petrarch and Boccaccio had given their readers glimpses of a loveliness which they themselves could only dimly descry, but it was a loveliness, howsoever uncertain, that haunted the minds of succeeding scholars. Then, when this longing for the treasures of an earlier age had sufficiently fired the imagination of men, the first step was taken for its accomplishment by gathering together as many as might be found of the precious classic manuscripts. Eventually the secret of Greek and Latin composition was extorted from their silent pages, and the ancient tongues began to be written with the spontaneous ease and grace of a living language. But first the books had to be collected, then corrected, then

expounded. Not till all this had been done could
there be any familiarity with the well-turned
phrases of the classic mind, so different from
the mediæval mode. Of this age of acquisition,
three names stand out foremost in Florence:
Poggio Bracciolini, Leonardo Bruni, and Palla
Strozzi. Each in his turn roamed over Italy or
despatched agents worldwide to gather into one
and house, within the city, the scattered glories
of Greece and Rome. Poggio is credited with the
discovery of Quintilian's works and of certain of
the lost writings of Cicero, Lucretius, Plautus,
etc. Bruni was the great translator, whose ver-
sion of the *The Apologia* and other dialogues of
Plato and of the *Nicomachean Ethics* and *Politics*
of Aristotle were considered among the great
achievements of the time; while Palla Strozzi
is an earlier type of the literary patron which
Cosimo de' Medici was to make so fashionable
in Europe. These three besides may be looked
upon, in their several ways, as the founders of
the Florentine University which hardly flour-
ished till their day. In time their work would
blossom into most beautiful flowers of literature,
some strangely petalled, some of exotic loveliness, some perfumed and some utterly scentless,
or concealing beneath their extreme comeliness
a poisoned breath. But this was rather at a later
period when S. Antonino had passed away to his
rest. Simultaneously with this new birth in literature opened the Spring of the Arts according
to the graceful coloured allegory of Botticelli.
All the world was young again. The competition

for the second gates of the Florentine Baptistry in 1401 marks the beginning of Renaissance sculpture and brings into prominence the names of Brunelleschi, Donatello, and Ghiberti. Then arose another trinity of talent: Masaccio, Fra Angelico, and Fra Lippi, who dipped their brushes in the colour-box of nature and painted the visions that their souls had seen. Altogether a wonderful age, this dawn of the *Quattrocento*, with its strong piquant personalities in the realms of arts and letters, men who took up the mantle that had fallen from the shoulders of the earlier prophets. They were not quite so simple, so ingenuous, so religious-minded as were their fathers, not quite so convinced of the value of the *dolce stil nuovo*, not quite so full of the eager optimism that gave such moving life to the writings and achievements of their immediate predecessors. It is true that they were entering into the kingdom of knowledge, but also, inevitably, into the kingdom of doubt. Where the sunlight is brighter, there are the darker shadows.

And there were shadows enough to be found in Florence. The political and constitutional history of this city is a difficult and intricate affair. There is no place here to stop and disentangle its threads. In a passage of bitterness, the exiled Dante addresses thus this "most famous and most beautiful daughter of Rome":

Thou who makest such fine-spun
Provisions that to middle of November
Reaches not what thou in October spinnest,

How oft within the time of thy remembrance
Laws, money, offices and usages
Hast thou remodelled, and renewed thy members?
And if thou mind thee well and see the light,
Thou shalt behold thyself, like a sick-woman
Who cannot find repose upon her down
But by her tossing wardeth off her pain.[1]

This simile sketches with sufficient clearness the unhealthy, restless constitution-making that went on perpetually in Florence. Perhaps, however, the poet is too hard in his judgment on this wayward republic. The problem was in a manufacturing city to establish an artisan democracy. This in itself was difficult enough, but when viewed in its circumstances in Florence became downright impossible. For the landed nobility needed a strong hand to keep them in check, a work for which a democratic form of government is eminently unfitted. Democracy again seemed hopeless when faced by such an expansive empire as Florence was now acquiring. Athens had failed, Carthage had crumbled, and Rome had changed her republican institutions, when they found themselves developing into an imperial State, for the harmonising of freedom and sovereign-sway needs such nice adjustment as the mob or crowd or *demos* is too clumsy to achieve. Efficiency and success in such

---

[1] Dante Alighieri, *Purgatorio*. in *The Divine Comedy*, trans. Henry Wadsworth Longfellow (Leipzig: Berhard Tauchnitz, 1867), Canto 6, lines 142–151.

an undertaking seem to require an oligarchy or a princedom. To this separation of interests between an agricultural gentry outside Florence and a commercial commonwealth within, was added, apparently, a racial distinction; for all the Florentine Chroniclers declare that the nobility were Teutonic and the burghers Italic. Moreover, the great mediæval party-cry had been raised not in vain in the city, where Ghibelline feudal lords and Guelfic merchants fought continually in the streets. These were three deep-rooted, inevitable causes of discord, and their effect was heightened by artificial checks and balances which, intended originally to prevent the legislature or the executive from becoming arbitrary, ended by paralysing all the forces of government. Thus the Signory and the Colleges could block each other's designs; and the *Parte Guelfa* (formed to prevent any Ghibelline disturbance and ostensibly distinct from government, in reality the driving power of government) complicated the situation by its anomalous position in which it divorced power from responsibility.

So that by the end of the Fourteenth Century the people were ruled by a close democracy which was practically an aristocracy, or rather a veiled kingship, vested in a single family. In our Saint's youth, this organised machinery of sovereignty was in the hands of the Albizzi, but it was soon captured by the Medici, who continued and developed this system of despotism. It is clear then that S. Antonino was born into a city distracted by factions, divided by legislature and executive artificially, set in opposition, filled with an artisan population at once manufacturing and commercial, and guided by a band of merchant princes whose banks sometimes held in fee whole kingdoms (as when Edward III pawned England to the Bardi for 1,365,000 gold florins), yet who in speech, dress, and theoretic political power were hardly at all raised above the citizens they employed. Finally it must be noted that out of a population of about 90,000 inhabitants, only 4,000 possessed the franchise. Such a state of social disorganisation was bound to be reproductive of terrible evils, economic and moral.

But the chief cause of the moral evils that then afflicted Florence, has been traced to the Great Pestilence, which came down on Europe in 1348. Travelling from the East, its arrival could be predicted almost exactly in its even deliberate march across the Western world. Its suddenness, the unmistakable nature of its symptoms, the irresistibleness of its attack, the wholesale destruction it effected have caused its horror to be stamped across the literature of the Fourteenth Century. On the English writers of that period, on Langland, Chaucer, Wycliffe, who witnessed it in their most impressionable years, falls a hush, the silence of terror. Still from the graphic pages of Boccaccio a dreadful picture of its dissolving force can be seen. It broke up the social structure of Europe by the swift removal of one third of its population. It stunned men, through their feeling of complete helplessness, into a feverish disregard of all moral law.

Moreover the terrible mortality in the monasteries made the religious superiors eager to fill up the vacant places. Any who presented themselves were accepted, boys, unlettered, inefficient. The strength of the rule was diluted, its standard lowered to encourage these novices to persevere. Fasts were forgotten, poverty disappeared, the Divine Office was neglected. Then on the heels of all this distress came the terrible Schism of the West, when the faithful saw two, eventually three, claimants to the Papacy disputing the obedience of the Nations. This second horror was even more appalling than the first. S. Catherine of Siena wrote in a letter: "For everything else like war, dishonour, and other tribulations would seem less than straw in comparison with this."[2] Religious Orders were also divided by this two-edged sword, and with this division came a further lessening of all effectual control by superiors over their subjects. The Order of S. Dominic, the history of which must enter necessarily in a biography of this kind, was also split into two obediences, with the same inevitable result. "It has altogether run wild," says S. Catherine in another place.[3] But in 1390, Bl. Raymund of Capua, her "Father and Son" as she

---

[2] Vida D. Scudder, ed., trans., *Saint Catherine of Siena as Seen in Her Letters* (London: J. M. Dent & Sons, LTD., 1911), 264.

[3] Ibid., 123.

called him, was elected to the headship of that
portion of it which remained faithful in its allegiance to the Roman line of Pontiffs. With him
came in the quickening life of reform. A few
earnest friars, here and there, were struggling
to bring back animation to the wasted and sti-
fled form of religion; but their efforts, however
well-directed, failed in concentration. They could
affect little except in their immediate environment. But the new Master General rallied the
forces, unified them and thus intensified their
power for good.

Foremost among these Paladins of Observance
was the Bl. Giovanni Dominici, a Florentine,
born in 1350, who became a Dominican in
1367, was nominated subsequently Cardinal of
S. Sisto and Archbishop of Ragusa, and died
in 1419 in Bohemia, Legate for the Holy See.
Commissioned in 1391 by Raymund of Capua,
he went to the Priory of S. Domenico in Venice,
there to restore religious discipline. From this
dates the beginning of Dominican reform. From
there Dominici passed to Città di Castello in
Umbria, to Fabiano in the March of Ancona,
and to S. Domenico in Cortona. But his presence
will be noted in these pages rather for his work
in Fiesole.

Here he began about 1400 a Church and
Convent for the friars of his Order who desired
to live up to the full, strict observance as laid
down in the Dominican Constitutions. It was
the beginning of the famous congregation of

Lombardy, which for its austerity, its piety, its poverty, no less than for the splendour of its Churches and the brilliancy of its members, sheds an extraordinary lustre on the Order of S. Dominic. There are names in it that dazzled their contemporaries and from which the glory among the children of men has not yet departed, for besides the Bl. Giovanni Dominici, one may cite S. Antonino, Fra Angelico, Fra Bartolomeo, and Girolamo Savonarola.

From the summit of the hill of Fiesole one looks down upon the gay City of Flowers. It lies at one's feet an entrancing sight, cut across in its south-western corner by the silver band of the sacred Arno, while out from its centre, amid spires and marble palaces, "whispering from her towers the last enchantments of the middle ages," rises the fairy dome of her Cathedral, than which Michelangelo could conceive upon earth nothing more beautiful. From this high chosen hill, how often must the Bl. Giovanni have gazed upon the city of his birth. How many a tie of memory linked up its fortunes in the past with the Order to which he belonged. How S. Maria Novella in its chaste loveliness seemed to call to him across the valley, while he thought of its walls, frescoed, under the matchless guidance of Fra Jacopo Passavanti, with the Dominican ideal of Church and State. How different was that high-wrought theory of the dual monarchy, a Papal Emperor and an Imperial Pope together marshalling the forces of the world, from the sad reality of a cross-purposed Christendom, plague-stricken and torn by schism. Who knows whether or not there came to him a glimpse of the "vision splendid"? Perhaps the Ancient of Days drew back for a moment the veil that shrouded the future round about and to comfort and encourage his servant vouchsafed an Apocalypse. Perhaps through the haze of the future, he saw our great Archbishop "the Father of his people"; and gazed at the gentle form of Fra Angelico; and heard the thunder-tones of Savonarola, prophet and martyr; and watched the perfect painting of Fra Bartolomeo, softened by the depths of human friendship that its lines reveal; and listened to the graceful eloquence of Fra Benedetto da Foiano, the last heroic prior of S. Maria Novella. Who knows or who can tell how far he saw in prophecy the things that were to be hereafter?

He was to pass away, to end his work and be gathered to the saints, but not until he had handed on to another the sacred fire that had been enkindled in his own heart and had prepared the way for another, greater, to come after him, one of those outstanding geniuses who mould the contours of the world, "for whom the eternal ages watch and wait."

II

Birth and Boyhood

THIS great disciple of Bl. Giovanni Dominici, who was to excel beyond all the dreams of his master, was born in the Via del Cocomero, now named the Via Ricasoli, after a Florentine hero of United Italy. The street stretches from the Duomo to the Piazza di S. Marco. This coincidence is striking; for it may be broadly reckoned that the life of S. Antonino is separated off into two divisions, as a Dominican and as a Prelate, as Prior of S. Marco and as Archbishop in the Duomo. Between these two centres was he born. The old house has gone long since to make room for public buildings and palaces, and the new street with its new-fangled name seems to have no sympathy with its old associations. And yet it has—as indeed every street and almost every stone of Florence must have—its own quaint and choice story to tell. Its corner, as one turns into it from the Via di Pucci, is gay with a much weather-stained shrine, holding a Madonna attributed to Filipino Lippi and another assigned to Buffalmacco. Certainly in this street lived Buffalmacco, the riotous, jovial artist whose humorous misdemeanours are part of the stock-in-trade of every Florentine cicerone. Giotto again graced it with his presence;

and to it in 1466 came old Donatello to die, in a house given him by Piero il Gottoso, the son and successor of Cosimo de' Medici. Here again lived Bonaventura, the husband of Bianca Capello, over whose pathetic personality have not theatre-goers wept these many centuries? But more important still to S. Antonino was the nearness of the little street to the Palazzo dei Medici, now the Palazzo Ricardi. The original palace was only built in 1430 from a design of Michelozzo Michelozzi; but on the same spot the earlier Medici had lived whose names appear here and there in the history of Florence, always interfering on behalf of the popular party and quietly waiting their time till Cosimo could reap the harvest of all their sowing.

Curiously enough, Cosimo and S. Antonino were born in the same year. Trouble has been caused over this date by the eighteenth-century editors of the *Bullarium Ordinis Prædicatorum*,[4] who mention the birth of S. Antonino as taking place on March 1st, 1390. But the *Life of the Saint*, written from the Process of Canonization, says that he was born in the Pontificate of Urban VI. This contradiction (for Boniface IX was elected on November 22nd, 1389) has been a great joy to pedants who have fought over it gaily in tomes, now fortunately too heavy to be lifted and too dusty to be read.

---

[4] Domenicani, *Bullarium Ordinis Praedicatorum* (Rome: Ex Typographia Hieronymi Mainardi, 1732), vol. 4, 424.

But it is the genealogy of the Saint for which the pedants have had most regard; and the various accounts of it are certainly confusing. Still the learned work of Fra Serafino Loddi, published in 1731, is a final reply to all cavillers. This adventurous friar attacks all who confound the parentage of S. Antonino with that of the de Fritti or the del Frilla or the Piavano Arlotto, and most of all those worst of heretics who dare affirm that these three families are one. But we will pass by, in patience, all Fra Serafino's array of offensive artillery and learn simply what he has discovered. The Saint's father then, according to this biographer, was Ser Niccolo di Pierozo, a descendant of Forcione, one of the earliest-known citizens of Florence. Niccolo is said to have been well born, though Florence did not trouble much about that. It is even said that he was related to the Strozzi and the Medici, for in the account of a marriage that took place on November 25th, 1385, we find him present along with representatives of these families, and we are told that custom prescribed that only relations should be invited to weddings. In any case, Niccolo was well known in the city. He belonged to the Guild of Advocates, for his profession was that of a Notary Public. Four times over was he "Proconsulo" of his Art, and twice "Prior." In this last capacity he helped the Gonfalonier in governing the Republic. Three times he was married, first to Lotta di Giovanni in 1368, then to Tommasa di Cenni di Nucci in 1383, lastly to

Sandra di Duccio in 1395. It was the second wife who was the mother of S. Antonino. She brought her husband a dowry of 200 scudi and a house to the south-west of the Duomo, since incorporated in the Canons-Close. In 1400 we find S. Antonino entering into possession of this house, but when he became a Dominican, his father sold it and went back to live in the old home in the Via di Cocomero, which he bequeathed to the use of his third wife. The only other children mentioned in the will besides S. Antonino, to whom one third of the property was left, were Fernando, on whom a third also devolved, and a daughter Niccolosa, a sister of our Saint, married to Domenico di M. Giovanni di Cinoccio dell' Ossa, who was to receive the house when her step-mother should die.[5] The names of other brothers and sisters are quoted by various authors; but to none other at his death did Ser Niccolo leave any of his properties.

We know therefore a little about the father of S. Antonino; about his mother just nothing at all. The early biographers put us off with trite phrases about "pious and honest parents," but on the really interesting points about his early childhood, his homelife, his mother and her ways, they give us no details. It may be that with a reticence and a modesty, the appreciation of which our own times have altogether blunted, they considered these things too sacred for the

---

[5] Antonino, *Lettere di S. Antonino* (Firenze: Tipografia Berbèra, Bianchi e C., 1859), 189.

common report of men, and deliberately drew the veil across the sanctuary when the most intimate parts of life's mystic rites were being celebrated.

One trait of the little boy's character can be gleaned from his name. He was christened Antony and as such he is called in all official documents and by his more immediate biographers. But there is abundant evidence to show that he was known as Antonino, or Little Antony. No doubt he was slightly built, a delicate lad. There are signs enough of this for he suffered all his life from a terrible hernia and was always supposed to be threatened with consumption.[6] But he was not so ridiculously small in stature as late writers usually describe him to be, for when his coffin was opened in 1589, his skeleton was measured and found to be about five feet and a half. It was not his size or physique which made him "Antonino," but rather, one cannot help feeling, that the little fellow was one of those children to whom instinctively such names of endearment are given, a lovable boy, with an attractive face.[7] Perhaps, too, the fact that he lost a mother's care before he was six years old made the neighbours pity him and give him that title of affection, under which we now invoke him.

---

[6] Societe des Bollandistes, *Acta Sanctorum*, vol. 14, *Maii, Tomus 1* (Paris: Société des Bollandistes, 1886), 319.
[7] Leonard Ser-Uberti, "Notes," in *Acta Sanctorum*, ed. Société des Bollandistes, vol. 14: *Maii, Tomus 1*, (Paris: Société des Bollandistes, 1886), 332.

In the early accounts of his childhood we find notices that imply that he was sent to school, but his delicate health caused his studies to be very broken. He tells us: "I confess that I have had no master in grammar, except when I was a little boy and he was a sorry teacher; nor in any other study except in dialectics and that was a very much interrupted course."[8] How the rest of his boyhood was spent we have no record. The Bull of Canonization speaks of his love of prayer and the strange fascination that preaching had for him. His favourite haunt was the splendid shrine of Orsanmichele, where his daily prayer of an hour naturally attracted attention. This wonderful tabernacle, which the superb genius of Orcagna had devised, had been finished about forty years earlier; but the boy came on no artistic pilgrimage. At any rate, modern tradition points out as the centre of his veneration an old wooden crucifix, formerly attached to one of the pillars, now hidden away behind a curtain to the right of the shrine.

Like all children, he was fond of watching processions; and especially was he attracted to those of the Dominican Church of S. Maria Novella. A true Florentine, he was always to be found in some church or shrine that was famous as a work of art. Orsanmichele represents in Florence the dawn of the Renaissance; S. Maria Novella the

---

[8] Antonino, *Summa Theologica Moralis* (Verona: P. and B. Ballerini, 1740), vol. 1, 3.

evening glow of the Middle Ages. Born of the Middle Ages, dying in the Renaissance, he found in himself, as did all Florence, the meeting of these two epochs. The music both of nature and supernature, of paganism and revealed faith, of the beauty of the human form and the loveliness of the soul found their echoes in his heart. He would wonder at the gorgeousness of Orcagna's work and then go back to the chaste simplicity of the Dominican architecture. There he would linger as the processions went by, kneeling among the jostling crowd, watching for his father to pass in his robes of office and choosing from among the variously clothed religious—as has done perhaps every Catholic boy—the Order to which, when he was grown up, he would belong.

Just as S. Antonino was reaching that most mysterious age of boyhood, which lies between the ignorance of the child and the full knowledge of the man, when the world begins to perplex and to thrill, when innocence stands puzzled on the threshold of hot life, there came "over the rim of his horizon" the figure of Giovanni Dominici, who was beginning his priory of strict observance on the lower slopes of the hill of Fiesole. Our Saint calls him "that splendid and wonderful hero who drew me to him by the brilliant ideas that sparkled in his sermons";[9] and he goes on to describe the style

---

[9] Antonino, *Historia vel Chronicon* (Lyons: N.p., 1543), vol. 3, 23, 11.

of his preaching: "One Lent course, I remember seeing an immense crowd of enthusiastic hearers in the Duomo listening to him as he explained the psalms, verse by verse, returning in the evening to hear him expound the Epistles of S. Paul. His style was grave and majestic. His voice rang clear like a trumpet call, never raised excessively nor lowered over-much, but extraordinarily impressive and full of force. Nor was it simply a matter of intellectual discourses, but of moving addresses that softened the most obdurate of hearts. Scarcely ever did he quote the philosophers or poets, but it was from the written Word of God, the book of the Scriptures, that he drew his appeals, which were enlivened with the wonderful freshness of his illustrations." In this brief account by S. Antonino one can understand the influence that the preaching of such a master had over the reserved boy, drawing him to new ideals. It was the character of the man much more than the words he spoke that made him so magnetic a centre for the young Florentines.

"There was nothing severe about him," continues the Saint, "nothing harsh, and he had a wonderful gift for detecting character. None came to him with any sorrow but went away consoled. In intellectual matters he could explain the most intricate questions with such astonishing clearness and could touch them about with so much of his own gentleness and sweetness, that difficulties vanished or at least no longer continued to distress. His dress was always humble, his presence grave and majestic, his stature tall, his person handsome, his face dignified yet remarkable for its pleasantness. He was invariably honest and straightforward; he never intrigued nor was in any sense insincere; yet his simplicity never allowed him to be outwitted by the craft or cunning of others. Gold and silver were never in his possession; and even his books were only such as he found in the Priories where he stayed."[10]

After the disturbing influence of the Plague and the moral upheaval caused by the schism, Florence, always a religious city, welcomed so worthy a friar who was moreover by birth one of her own citizens. His brilliant yet devout discourses, his fine manly character, his personal austerity and pleasing presence were all such as would appeal to the Tuscan temperament. Not for a long time had any one come who so united in himself what was best in the early dawning Renaissance with what was venerable and clothed with majesty in the eventide of Mediævalism.

The boy Antonino, "grave, gentle, silent,"[11] left lonely by his mother's death, wandering from Orsanmichele to S. Maria Novella, praying, joining in processions, studying by himself, reading as long as his delicate health allowed, appealing

---

[10] Antonino, *Chronicon*, iii., 23, ii.

[11] Francis Castiglione, "Life," in *Acta Sanctorum*, ed. Société des Bollandistes, vol. 14: *Maii, Tomus 1*, (Paris: Société des Bollandistes, 1886), 318.

by his refined beauty to the passers-by, lovingly
called a pet-name by all the world, was just the
one to be taken captive by such an ideal, clothed
in so appropriate a personality.

One hot day then in mid-summer, the little
pilgrim walked out to the temporary Priory that
peered down upon Florence from the flank of
the Tuscan hills.

Fiesole had of old founded Florence; Florence
was now going back, up the gentle slope, to its
mother Fiesole.

III

The Young Dominican

THIS hot summer's day in 1404[12] seemed to end fruitlessly. The boy had thought to take the decisive step which should place him among the ranks of God's priests, for he had made up his mind to ask for the habit of S. Dominic from the hands of Fra Giovanni. It was with that design that he was leaving behind his home in Florence and mounting the hill to Fiesole.

We do not know whether the two had spoken together before or not. It seems unlikely, for S. Antonino mentions only the preaching of Dominici as having been the attraction. Now, however, they met. Fra Giovanni questioned him about his vocation, his motives, and his mental and spiritual fitness for the religious life. "And Antonino," says his earliest biographer, "seemed to this man a boy of good parts and of excellent disposition, yet of tender age withal and delicate health, and so he bade him wait a few years until he should be better able to bear the austerities of a religious Order."[13] After his experience of

---

[12] This date seems rather more easy than any other to reconcile the conflicting statements of the biographers. But it is impossible to be at all positive.

[13] Castiglione, "Life," 319.

the laxity introduced into the cloister through
accepting subjects for whom the rule had to be
exceedingly relaxed, the good Dominican was
forced to be more than ordinarily prudent in
his choice of novices. The Convent was as yet
unbuilt, there were no other postulants, and the
lad looked slightly made and unable to undergo
the full routine of Dominican life. Moreover, Fra
Giovanni was himself of an extremely robust
constitution, preaching, we are told, sometimes
five times a day without feeling it to be any tax
upon his strength.[14] So this too probably helped
him to decide against receiving Antonino. But
when he gave the boy this refusal, a wistful look
in the little face at the rebuff touched the heart
of the friar, and more with the idea of comfort-
ing him than with any very definite intention, he
enquired what was his favourite study. "Canon
Law," replied the child. "Very well then," said Fra
Giovanni, "go home, and when you have learnt
by heart the whole *Decretal of Gratian* come to
me again."

It was characteristic of the quiet determination and indomitable spirit of the lad that without a word he turned away, quite contented with
the terms, though he must have known that
the *Decretal* was a bulky volume. He had however a definite promise now, and, as for his part
of the agreement, he had too firm a faith in the

---

[14] Societe des Bollandistes, *Acta Sanctorum*, vol. 22, *Iunii*,
Tomus 2, 399.

reality of his vocation to doubt that God who had begun the good work in him would accomplish it in His own good time. So he returned to his father's house in Florence and set to work at his formidable task. Page after page of the *Decretal* was learnt, and while the months went by his heart grew lighter, as he saw the number of the leaves that separated him from the end of his labours gradually lessening. But this was not his only preparation for his future life. Day by day the peasant women who came into the Church of Orsanmichele on their way to the marketplace or the numberless craftsmen that turned down towards the business centre of Old Florence, would point out to one another that grave young lad kneeling at the shrine who seemed already so deeply penetrated with the spirit of God and, like those who were witnesses of the childhood of S. John the Baptist, they would perhaps wonder in their hearts what manner of man this should be.

The only anxiety that seems at all to have troubled Antonino himself was the dread lest his feeble health should prove an obstacle to the fulfilment of his hopes, for the people used to tell him he would never be able to bear the discipline of this strict religious Order, and drew exaggerated pictures of the severities of the noviciate. But somehow the gentle boy grew quite convinced, though he said little, that if God called, the strength would be given. So indeed it proved. This delicate child lived to be an old man of seventy, though health and strength were never spared in the exercise of his apostolic and pastoral labours. Indeed his physical endurance became afterwards a constant wonder to his people.[15]

The only effect of these sinister prophecies was that the boy grew more determined to make these months a time of preparation for the fasts and mortifications of his future life. Nor was it difficult to find opportunities at home for this self-discipline. His parents, no doubt, knew of his purpose, but his stepmother did not cease to look anxiously after her little son, fearing lest in his desire for mortification he should still further weaken his broken health. But sometimes when she would pile up his plate with meat, Antonino, who wanted to accustom himself to the Dominican diet of fish, used to wait till she was busy with his other brothers and sisters, and throw his meat to the cats under the table. At least this is the tale told by one of his biographers,[16] though Antonino himself, who ought to have known best, only confessed to hiding the meat under his plate.[17] Perhaps even so, it got to the cats at last. But in any case, one feels sure that his innocent schemes were often enough discovered by one or other of his family circle, to his great confusion; and that the good mother would shake her head in mingled

---

[15] Castiglione, "Life," 322.

[16] Girolamo Razzi, *Vita Miracoli. e Traslazione di S. Antonino Arcivescovo di Firenze* (N.p.: 1589), 14.

[17] Castiglione, "Life," 319.

annoyance and admiration at the pertinacity of the quiet boy.

A year passed by with its daily recurring round of prayer and self-discipline, and the constant study of the task imposed on him, till at length the time came when Antonino, after repeated trials, one may be sure, felt certain that he knew the *Decretal* from end to end. For the second time he made the pilgrimage to Fiesole. Joy was in his heart for he could not doubt the promise made by Fra Dominici. Again then he found himself in the presence of the Dominican, explained his errand, announced that he had mastered by memory the crabbed pages of the Decretal, and begged for the habit as his coveted reward.

The holy prior must have been glad to see again the happy-looking child, older now by a year, yet still, we are persuaded, so frail and delicate. The quiet manner in which the boy had turned away resolutely to go back and conquer his Canon Law probably lingered in Fra Giovanni's remembrance, but it could scarcely have prepared him for such a power of memory and perseverance as he now found revealed in this lad of sixteen. Taking down the great volume of the *Corpus Juris*, he turned over the pages of the *Decretal*, asking Antonino first one distinction and then another without finding him at all at fault. "A kind of miracle," says the redactor of the Process of Canonization; "not without God's special light" echoes the Papal Bull.

At length the Bl. Giovanni shut the volume and told the expectant boy that he would no longer refuse him the habit. Then Antonino bade farewell to the world; and, once within the unfinished monastery, one stage in his life's history is over. God has called and he has obeyed. He has gone out from home, from his father's house, and has entered the cloister. For a while he is to be away from the busy crowds of Florence, its manufacture, its commerce, undisturbed by any sound save the mellowed tolling of the city's bells, yet knowing surely that one day he must go back, down the hill, step once more among the tumult and try to guide it Godwards.

But his stay at Fiesole was of short duration, for he left almost at once for Cortona. Here he passed his year of noviciate. While he was away, the Bishop of Fiesole, Jacopo d'Altoviti, gave land for the building of the Priory, which was begun in March, 1406. By September of the same year, we find record of a community of fourteen Dominicans settled in the Priory.[18] Just at this point, however, the order of the comings and goings of S. Antonino is rather difficult to unravel, so that it is only with much uncertainty that his progress can be followed. It seems probable, however, that when he returned from Cortona, he stayed with the Hermits of S. Jerome higher up on the hill of Fiesole. Then the

---

[18] Robert Langton Douglas, *Fra Angelico* (London: G. Bell and Sons, 1902), 23–24.

Infirmary was completed and in it the community dwelt for some time. But within a few weeks the rest of the building was got ready, and the whole conventual life was definitely established on September 29th, 1406. He was back, however, once more at Cortona during the ensuing year, where he was joined by two new novices, brothers, who have made names for themselves in the history of art: Fra Benedetto di Vicchio and Fra Giovanni, the latter of whom all the world now knows as Fra Angelico.

In 1408, the Convent, dedicated in honour of S. Dominic, was finished at Fiesole, so back again the novices came to their first home. There is a fragrance that always attaches to the springtime of things, when life begins fresh, radiant, and full of hope and promise. The early days, the first records, the primitive sources of things, the tumultuous origin of dynasties are the periods round which gather legends and myths. Even the places where rise the great and famous rivers have been consecrated by pious tradition and deemed sacred by the custom of the race. So too has God dealt with His own people. The early stories of Church History, the rise of Religious Orders, the first conversions of great peoples are exceedingly hallowed. And so was it with the Convent of Fiesole. At this date the novice-master was Fra Lorenzo di Ripafratta (beatified by Pius IX in 1851); while among the novices were S. Antonino, Fra Pietro Capucci and Fra Costanzo di Fabiano (both beatified by Pius VII in 1811), and Fra Angelico whom all the world has put among the Saints.[19]

But public events soon broke up the little band. It must not be forgotten that the Great Schism of the West was still raging. For a long time Florence had clung to the Roman line of Pontiffs; but when Innocent VII died on Nov. 6th, 1406, the Republic sent the Bl. Giovanni to Rome to protest against the election of a new Pope. It seemed to the Magistracy that now that the Roman claimant was dead the easiest way to end the Schism was to summon a General Council of the Church, at it to gather together the adherents of both allegiances, and then proceed to the election of an undoubted Pope. But the Cardinals of the Roman obedience saw that if this were done the power would be taken out of their own hands. By themselves they could, of course, choose whom they would; elsewhere their influence would be lost amid the combined votes of all the Cardinals created by the rival Pontiffs. Hence by the end of the month they chose as their candidate Angelo Corrario, who took the name of Gregory XII. Some efforts were made by Gregory and the Antipope Benedict XIII to come to terms at Savona; but each was too much afraid of appearing to recognize the other,

---

[19] W. H. Lecky speaks of the "angelic friar of Fiesole"; as a "saint who may be compared with any in the hagiology." W. H. Lecky, *History of the Rise and Influence of the Spirit of Rationalism in Europe* (London: Longmans, Green & Co., 1910), vol. 1, 26.

and in the end they never met. By this time a general disgust was felt all over Europe at the protracted length of the Schism; and the scheme was mooted for summoning a General Council, as Florence had proposed, which should represent the two obediences, should depose the rival Popes, and proceed to the election of a third. The result was the Council of Pisa, held under Florentine protection, but acknowledged and favoured by France and England. The Council opened on March 25th, 1409. Both Gregory and Benedict banned its proceedings; but they were deposed by their recalcitrant Cardinals, and their place taken by Pietro Filargo, O.S.F., Archbishop of Milan, under the title of Alexander V. As a matter of fact this expedient disturbed still further the peace of Christendom, for there was now a third claimant to the unique See of Peter.

Florence, of course, accepted the new Pope. He indeed owed his position to her initiative and support. But the little Priory of Fiesole, under the leadership of Giovanni Dominici, clung to the Roman obedience; so the whole community, owing to the persecution it suffered from the Magistracy, had to make off to some place of safety as best it could, and its property returned to the Bishop of Fiesole. As far as can be gathered, S. Antonino went with the others to Foligno and thence, on account of a plague in that city, again to Cortona in 1413. Here he was elected Prior in 1417; and then successively within the next few years to the same position at

Naples, Gaeta, and Siena. But it is almost impossible at present to date precisely each term of
office. In 1424, he made a canonical visitation of
the Dominican Priory at Naples, and in 1430 he
was Prior of S. Maria sopra Minerva in Rome,
where he was present at the translation of the relics of S. Catherine of Siena. At the same time he
served as an Auditor of the Rota in the Pontifical
Court (where his favourite study of Canon Law
stood him in good stead). In this capacity he is
said to have reformed the salaries of the Notaries
Apostolic.[20] But the whole chronology of his life
at this period and for the next few years is, as
we have said, exceedingly perplexing. The only
other office held by him that we shall mention
here is that of Vicar-General of the Reformed
Congregation of Strict Observance—a group of
Priories linked up with the Convent of Fiesole.
His term of office ended in 1442; but he was
re-elected in 1445.

These are the few, isolated facts, which have
fallen through the sieve of history. How he ruled
his Priories, the innovations he introduced, the
buildings he erected, the reforms he effected—all
these things have been left unrecorded and are
forgotten, or at least for the present are lost to
us. An anecdote might perhaps have given, as by
a flash, some light on his character at this period.
But, as it is, the vague and colourless remarks of

---

[20] Antonino, *Summa Theologica Moralis*, vol. 3, 6, 3, 3, 272;
Card. Lucca Opera xv., pars. ii., d. 32 de Rota, n. 3.

his pious biographers could be applied to any
Saint of any century in any Church. They are
bound to be so true that we cannot trust them.
They apply no doubt to S. Antonino, but only in
so far as he is like any other God-fearing man,
not (and surely this is the proper work of the
biographer) where he differs from them.

And yet perhaps it is as well, for his entrance
now upon the scene is made the more dramatic
after the long silence and the hidden life. The
years have borne their fruit. He suddenly comes
before our notice with a new greatness, a trans-
formed personality. No longer the delicate, affectionate boy whose attractive beauty and charm
of manner made him lovable to his fellows, he
appears now as a man amid men, dealing in
Florence with her terrible woes, in intimate
intercourse with her hard but magnificent ruler,
a friend of Popes and Emperors and Eastern
Patriarchs, a theologian among the Church's official delegates, yet living a life of simple austerity and knit in bonds of love with Fra Angelico,
gentlest of Dominicans.

IV

At S. Marco

THE Council of Pisa, it will be remembered, affected the Schism rather for evil than for good. It only succeeded in adding one more claimant to the Throne of the Vicar of Christ. But the idea of a General Council still appealed to a great number of influential men who considered that it had not had a fair chance of producing its proper effect. Especially did this view find a passionate exponent in the person of the Emperor Sigismund, whose bustling activity (as has not seldom happened in the Teutonic line of Cæsars) was much attracted by the old ideal of the European hegemony invested in the Imperial dignity. He saw here a chance for setting forth dramatically his leadership of Christendom; and it must be frankly admitted that whatever success the subsequent Council obtained was due in large measure to his initiative and support.

The Council met at Constance on November 1st, 1414. Its earlier sessions consisted principally of doctrinal discussions concerning the orthodoxy of the Bohemian school of teachers, ending in the condemnation and death of Huss. Then after almost a year had passed without very much being effected, Sigismund in his quixotic way set out on a tour through Europe to pacify

warring kings and gain their adherence to the
Assembly. As often happened in these chivalrous days, his romantic quest, though it failed
in its immediate purpose, succeeded in its more
ambitious aims. He secured for the Council the
support of public opinion. The Roman Pope
sent Giovanni Dominici, now a Cardinal, and
the Condittore Prince Carlo Malatesta (an
oddly assorted, yet really representative pair) as
his *Legates*, who, in his name, renounced all his
dignities and declared his willing acceptance
of whomsoever the Council should elect. John
XXIII had already been summarily deposed, and
Benedict XII, whose pretensions were a legacy of
Pisa, lived in his Spanish Castle, undaunted but
impotent. On November 11th, 1417, Cardinal
Oddo Colonna was chosen Pope and at once
assumed full power under the title of Martin V.

This election was indeed justified by its
results. After this protracted Schism of forty
years, the union of the Church was immediately effected. One of its lesser consequences (for
Florence accepted the new Pontiff who took up
his residence in her midst) was the return of the
Dominicans to Fiesole. They came back in 1418.
The Bishop once more made over to them the
Priory of San Domenico, on condition of receiving from them in exchange a sacred vestment
said to be worth 200 ducats. This was paid for out
of moneys left to S. Antonino by his father, who
had just died. Another trace of the re-occupation
of the Fiesole Convent is the handiwork of

Fra Angelico, who began at once to display his
talents in the decoration of Church and Priory.
During these years of labour at Fiesole (1418–
1435) the artist-friar was finding his way out
from the conventions of the early schools into the
freedom and "naturalness" of the modern critics.
His monastic life cut him off from the delights
of home and the warm affection of a family, but
the loving nature that God had given him found
its vent in portraying, almost for the first time in
Christian art, the Motherhood of Mary and the
Childhood of her Son, for his Madonnas have
the true movements of nature and his Christ has
all the emotions of an affectionate boy. The beauties of Earth too appealed to him, as they had
seldom before to other painters, with a full and
unaffected delight; and his visions of Heaven
are so wonderfully ideal, because they are tran-
scribed from a faithful rendering of Earth, "the
manuscript of God":

> Ordina quest' amore,
> O tu che m'ami.

Florence at this date touched the full height
of all her splendour, in the content of her citizens
and the grandeur of her achievements. Under
the Medici, it is true, her influence was greater
in the political scale of Europe; even her artistic
value may have been intensified through the brilliant band of painters, sculptors, and architects,
to whom the discerning patronage of Cosimo
and his house gave such great opportunities. Yet

measured rather by the happiness of the people and the personal worth and variety of her men of art and letters, the Government at this period, says Guicciardini, was the wisest, most glorious, and happiest that ever the city had seen. And Vespasiano Bisticci, another contemporary and a devout panegyrist of the Medici, bore the same witness: "In that time, from 1422 to 1433, the City of Florence was in a most blissful state, abounding with excellent men in every faculty, and it was full of admirable citizens."[21]

Yet just then occurred one of those violent changes in Florentine government which were so common in her history. The carefully matured, but unobtrusive power of the Medici, which up to this time had appeared only fitfully, seems to have scared the Albizzi, who then held the chief rule of the city. By a sudden appeal to the people, a provisional government was appointed which banished Cosimo and his friends to various cities of Europe. But the recoil was equally violent. Within a year, Cosimo returned ("by divine providence" says S. Antonino[22]), this time to a practically unlimited power, "on the shoulders of all Italy." Officially he was only one of the city Magistrates, he bore no exceptional command and assumed no newly devised office. He continued the same forms of government—or nearly so, simply narrowing the number of officials, and

---

[21] Vespasiano da Bisticci, *Vite di Uomini Illustri del Secolo XV* (Firenze: Barbèra, Bianchi e comp., 1859).

[22] Antonino, *Chronicon*, vol. 3, tit. XXII, fol. CXXX, IX, b.

carefully depriving them of all power. Above all, he attempted to rule Florence by dazzling her with such splendour (not personal, but civic) as his vast wealth made possible. Cynically enough, he admitted his use of the arts to be but an instrument of government: "I know the humours of this city, fifty years will not pass before we are driven out; but the buildings will remain." He spoke truly. Five hundred years have passed away and still the whole architecture of Florence rings with the name of the Medici.

To one of these buildings we must now turn.

The fame of the Dominicans of Fiesole instigated the parishioners of S. George-beyond-the-Arno to request them on June 9th, 1435, to make a foundation in their parish. The Prior of S. Domenico accepted the offer and sent some of his community to establish the new colony. But the site proved ill-suited for their work, as it was too far out from the centre of the city. In consequence, the Priors of the Arts (the official rulers of Florence) petitioned the Pope to transfer the Dominicans to the Church and Monastery of S. Marco, which till then had belonged to the Silvestrians. Eugenius IV immediately agreed to the proposal, issuing a Bull to order the unfortunate Silvestrian monks to exchange S. Marco for S. Georgio. Here Cosimo de' Medici saw a golden opportunity for once more entrenching his position among the people. The Order was reformed, and therefore was popular with the Pontifical Court; it was no less popular in

Florence as the petition of the Priors bore witness. He therefore offered to rebuild the whole block, Church and monastery as well. His offer was gladly accepted by the Vicar-General of the Lombard Congregation, who was no other than S. Antonino, then living at Fiesole. The plans for the new Priory were put up for competition, and the design of Michelozzo was preferred.[23]

Thus began the building of S. Marco. In 1439, the great library was finished and enriched by the four hundred precious manuscripts which Niccolo Niccoli had bequeathed to the city. Cosimo, too, frequently gave huge sums of money to make the collection of books still more valuable—in 1444 allowing 400 gold florins to purchase books on Canon Law, and in 1445 adding 250 more for buying theological writings. It was, too, in 1439 that S. Antonino was made first Prior of S. Marco, an office that he held conjointly with the Priorship of Fiesole till 1445, when a separation between the two was made; at the same time, he appears to have continued in his post as Vicar over all the Priories that were grouped together under the title of the Lombard Congregation. He it was, then, who welcomed Eugenius IV in 1443 when he came to the consecration of the Church on Epiphany Day, and the friendly Pontiff dined, supped, and slept at S. Marco, returning next morning to the other Dominican Priory in Florence, S. Maria Novella.

---

[23] *Antonino, Chronicon*, Tit. XXII., fol. CXL., x., 5.

Another triumph for Florence, and one in which S. Antonino again took part, had occurred shortly before. In 1439, the Council of Ferrara, convoked in order to deliberate on the Union of East and West, was on account of the plague transferred to Florence. The citizens found in their midst their own spiritual chief, Pope Eugenius, and from the East the Emperor whose fame and supposed magnificence were legends bequeathed from the Crusading times. The Patriarch, too, of Constantinople, who claimed an equal jurisdiction with the Pontiffs of the West, had journeyed in his venerable age to assist at the re-union of the Churches. There were gathered together the most renowned prelates of Europe and Asia, their most consummate theologians, and the representatives of the Christian princes. Among the rest figures the name of S. Antonino. What his precise work was we do not know. We learn only that he was present, that he spoke, and that his learning and acumen took the fancy of the Pope.[24]

Although the most important result of the first meeting in a European city of Pope and Patriarch and Emperor was naturally enough the healing of the Schism that for so many centuries had rent Christendom apart, other effects were produced on the Florentines. They laughed at the fantastic hats and loose, Eastern

---

[24] Mandell Creighton, *A History of the Papacy During the Period of the Reformation* (London: Longmans, Green & Co., 1882), vol. 2., 504.

robes and painted eyebrows of these unwonted Bishops from the Greek Empire; they were disappointed at the personal ignorance which these prelates showed of Homer and Hesiod, Plato and Aristotle; still, on the whole, they were overcome with respect for these strangers for whom the antique speech of the gods was a living language. Even in the pages of S. Antonino's works, the same process is noticeable. At first overpowered by the personal influence of Giovanni Dominici,[25] we find him decrying the study of the classics or at least depreciating their value; but in his later writings, he treats them much more kindly. That the pagan authors were scandalous in their lives, he does not to the last deny: "But this should not blind us to the truth of much that they have written, for truth wheresoever found is ever the truth of God."[26]

---

[25] Cf. Giovanni Dominici, *Locula Noctis*, ed. by Remi Coulon (Paris: A. Picard, 1908).

[26] Antonino, *Summa Theologica Moralis*, vol. 1, i., 3–4, 37.

V

The Good Archbishop

FLORENCE had thus for long been full of pageantry. It had housed Martin V when he came to his pontificate,[27] and had found himself without temporal support, until the ribald rhymes of the children about him made his stay there no longer possible. It had in its noble pity petitioned for the Antipope John XXIII to be made a Cardinal, and, when within a year of his doing reverence to Pope Martin, he passed out of life, it buried him with full splendour in the famous Baptistry of S. John. Thither too had Eugenius come for recognition. He had pacified the distracted city, decreed exile to the Albizzi, and brought back the Medici to their princedom. He had also with astonishing pomp himself consecrated and set in order the Cathedral, had held within its walls the most splendid bravery of the Latin obedience, and the still more striking grandeur[28] of the old decaying Eastern Cæsars and their Patriarchs, and had witnessed, along with a noble throng of Cardinals and Bishops the consecration of that monument of Medicean glory, the Priory of S. Marco. At

---

[27] Antonino, *Chronicon*, Tit. XXII., ii., fol. CXXX., b.
[28] Creighton, *Papacy*, vol. 1, 190.

this last ceremony he had been extraordinarily impressed with the frescoes of Fra Angelico. The strength and originality of their design and their artistic fearlessness were especially pleasing to him for they were informed with a distinctive Christian Faith. Consequently on his return to Rome in 1444, he took the artist-friar with him.

Within a year of their arrival occurred the death of Zabarella, Archbishop of Florence. The question at once came up of filling this important See; and it may be presumed that it was of especial interest to Eugenius, who knew so well Florence and all its extensive needs. For nine months (*Castiglione*, p. 319) the Pontiff hesitated. Then, on the advice of certain religious, he was reminded of S. Antonino, whose goodness and character he had long known. At once the Pope agreed and manifested his decision by appointing the Prior of S. Marco to the Archbishopric. But the story, as told by Vasari, though certainly inaccurate in details and perhaps even inaccurate in its main idea, is too well-known to be easily omitted here: "And because Fra Giovanni (Fra Angelico) seemed to the Pope, as he was indeed, a man of most holy life, gentle and modest, when the Archbishopric of Florence fell vacant, he adjudged him worthy of the rank; but the said friar hearing of it prayed His Holiness to give it to another, because he did not feel himself to be apt at governing men, and said that his Order had another friar, loving to the poor, learned, skilled in government and God-fearing whom the dignity would much better become than it would him. The Pope, hearing this and perceiving that what he said was true, granted him the favour, and so Fra Antonino of the Order of Preaching Friars was made Archbishop of Florence, a man of such holiness that he was canonised by Adrian VI in our own day."[29]

At any rate, by whatever means it had been brought about, S. Antonino was appointed to the See by the Pope. The Saint was on his way to make a visitation of the Priories of the Neapolitan kingdom when the news reached him of the Pope's appointment. His first thought was to avoid it by crossing over into Sardinia, but, while waiting in some town on the western seaboard among strangers who were not at all likely to recognise him, a nephew of his, Pietro by name, followed him to offer the congratulations of the family. The friar begged to be left alone, but the nephew, with all the determination of youth, declared that he would not leave his uncle's side. At last overcome by the persistence of the fellow, Antonino went on to Siena, with his mind still made up to refuse the dignity. But the Pope, hearing of his endeavour to escape and thereby still more convinced that he was the proper man for the post, despatched messengers to compel him to accept the Archbishopric and to repair immediately to Fiesole.

[29] Giorgio Vasari, *Stories of Italian Artists*, trans. E. L. Seeley (London: Chatto & Windus, 1906), 83; but Lapini (*Acta Sanctorum*, Maii, Tom. VII. 545) in 1569 denied completely that the See had first been offered to Fra Angelico.

Even when there, S. Antonino endeavoured to interest Cosimo de' Medici in his efforts at release; but Cosimo, knowing the popularity of the appointment, was the more anxious to give the impression that he had had, himself, a hand in the affair; so he wrote off to Rome desiring the Pope to hold to his decision.[30] When the news spread about Florence, the people were wild with joy. He was known already to be a strong-minded, fearless priest—in Fra Angelico's reputed words "loving to the poor and skilled in government." Moreover, the three previous prelates who had held the See since Martin V had raised it to an Archbishopric, had been absentees and foreigners, a Roman and two Paduans, whereas here was a Florentine, likely to live in his own city.

The Magistrates wrote lively letters to Fiesole urging S. Antonino to fear nothing and to take up his burden: "You love no doubt," say they, "the silence, the cloister, and the contemplation, but are we put here to live alone? Is it not rather true that the country to which we belong, the friends to whom we are bound by love, the social organisation in which we find ourselves, nay, the whole human race, have claims on us, and even rights over us?"[31] To a plea so impassioned and based on grounds of public utility and harder labours, the Saint could not be deaf.

---

[30] Société des Bollandistes, *Acta Sanctorum*, 321, n. 1.

[31] Cf. Antonino, *Lettere di S. Antonino*, 87–88; Giovanni Moro, *Di S. Antonino in Relazione alla Riforma Cattolica nel Secolo* XV, (Firenze: B. Seeber, 1899), 55–56.

He summoned to Fiesole the Abbots, Prelates, and chief men of the city, and there in their presence accepted the high office, begging in exchange their alms of prayer. His consecration took place in the Church of S. Domenico upon the hillside (the home of his novitiate) by Lorenzo Giocomini, O.P., Archbishop of Achaia, assisted by the two suffragans of the Archbishopric, Benozzo Federichi, Bishop of Fiesole, and Donato de' Medici, Bishop of Pistoja. Then on March 13th, 1446, the second Sunday in Lent, he came barefoot down the hill in the early morning light, which made the future scene of his life's work seem a wondrous thing of beauty. At the Church of S. Gallo outside the walls, he stayed to say his Mass, seeing in the sacrificial death of the Good Shepherd the model for his own pastorship; then he entered by the Gate of S. Gallo in the N.E. corner and down the east side of the city till he came to the Church of S. Pietro Maggiore, a little north of Sta. Croce. It exists no longer; but in it was performed, as Florentine custom dictated, the quaint mystic wedding of the Archbishop to his See, represented by the Abbess of the neighbouring Convent of the Benedictines, to whom he gave the ring. Then turning northwards again through the Borgo degli Albizzi, he came to the Duomo where the *Te Deum* was sung and S. Antonino spoke to his people. Then at last he reached his Palace and settled at once to his work.

The strenuous and austere Saint found himself thoroughly uncomfortable in his new home, or, for the word is misleading, not uncomfortable enough. He had to strike hard at the old ways before his conscience gave him rest. Numberless servants and hangers-on who fattened on revenues, not bequeathed for their use, were immediately dismissed. The tradition of fine living, which a nine-months' vacancy had done nothing to diminish, was rudely broken through. A friar by vow, energetic by nature or rather by force of habit, busy by office, he could not afford nor did he care for the *menu* of his predecessors. Moreover, he had accepted the post on the strength of the Gonfalonier's words that his people and the whole world had claims upon him, and he was in eager haste to acknowledge these claims. He declared that his money, his time, his strength, and his powers were henceforth at the mercy of his flock. At the same time, he entered on the path of reform. He found the Canons of the Cathedral lax in saying publicly the Divine Office, especially in the recitation of Matins at midnight. His efforts for long years were unavailing, but in 1456 he determined himself to attend regularly, although, in those days, the Palace did not abut on the Duomo, so that he had to walk down the street, while the Canons could reach the Choir without leaving cover. Canon Castiglione, his personal friend and his earliest biographer, tells how one snowy night in winter, when the sleet was sweeping down the deserted

streets, he and Mark, who both acted as the
Saint's secretaries, could not bring themselves to
venture out; but the Archbishop, leaving them
in bed, sallied forth alone across the open square
to the cold marble Cathedral, which must itself
have been like the wind-cave of Æolus. Another
work of his was to organise the studies of the
diocese, for the legacy of Plague and Schism had
been an ignorant clergy. He composed textbooks
on Church discipline, Canon Law; and from the
beginning of his episcopate started to plan out
the grand scheme of his monumental work on
Moral Theology.

Along with all this diocesan business, he had
on him the public burdens of his high office. We
find him sent as Ambassador to congratulate
Popes or to welcome Emperors. In 1452, when
Frederick III went to Rome with Eleonora to be
crowned, they passed through Florence. Here he
was met by S. Antonino and the full magistracy
of the city[32] and feasted with fitting solemnity.
But when the Emperor was leaving for Rome,
the citizens wanted the Archbishop to accom-
pany him and represent them at the ceremony.
This he refused. He was old, he said; and besides
he had a very poor opinion of Frederick: "There
was no sign in him of the Imperial dignity, nor
sense, nor wisdom, since he always had to get
others to do the talking for him. Instead he had
an excessive greed, always asking for presents

---

[32] Antonino, *Chronicon*, vol. 3, Tit. XXII., fol. CXLVI.,
xiii., 3

and joyfully accepting them. ... Eventually (says the Saint) he went home and left behind a very sorry name for character."

But at the election of Popes, S. Antonino was always willing to be of use to the Republic. He was sent with four other ambassadors to Pope Callixtus III in 1455. He treated that Pontiff to a learned address, rather mystical in spirit, for it mainly insisted on the supposed association between the name Callixtus and the word *callidus* (hot), which was intended to symbolise the Pope's zeal.[33] However pedantic it may sound to modern ears, the discourse was evidently quite in keeping with the oratorical fashion of that day, and created a sensation at the Roman Court.[34] On his return to Florence, the good Archbishop had to describe the whole function for the benefit of the citizens. They assembled in the Palace of the Signory, where he "told his battles o'er again." Here he found his wonderful memory, that had got him as a child into the Dominican Order, standing him in good stead. The whole affair had to be accurately and carefully detailed, and even his address had to be repeated for these Florentines, who had no other way of getting hold of a full report of the proceedings.[35]

But the most splendid reception of all was when he went with five other Legates of the

---

[33] Antonino, *Lettere*, 21, 189–191.

[34] Société des Bollandistes, *Acta Sanctorum*, 324.

[35] Antonino, *Chronicon*, vol. 3, Tit. XXII., cap. xiv.; Société des Bollandistes, *Acta Sanctorum*, 324.

most distinguished families of Florence—
Angelo Acciaioli, Luigi Guicciardini, Pietro
Pazzi, Guglielmo Rucellai, Pietro Francisco de'
Medici[36]—to salute the newly elected Pius II in
1458. The Saint was now an old man, with only
one year of life before him, and his reputation for
holiness, and still more, one may suppose, for his
wonderful powers of organization and his broad-
minded charity towards the poor, had made his
name almost a synonym for goodness in Italian
speech. Then, as now, he was known familiarly
as the "Good Archbishop." The tumultuous
throng of people to see him enter Rome and the
eagerness with which the Pontifical Court hastened to catch sight of him, gave much pleasure in Florence. Even in the city of the Popes
where one would think Bishops were a common
enough sight, it was noticed that crowds knelt
for his blessing and fought for the privilege of
kissing his hand or ring.[37] It was a premature
canonization, such as Nicholas V had declared
when he remarked that Antonino living was as
good a Saint as Bernardino dead.[38]

Old however as he was, and broken in health,
he made a great speech, if the account he gives
of it in his Chronicle[39] is anything like the

---

[36] Editor's note: Here, the author refers in short to Lorenzo
di Pierfrancisco de' Medici.

[37] Société des Bollandistes, *Acta Sanctorum*, 321.

[38] Ibid., 323

[39] Antonino, *Chronicon*, vol. 3, Tit. XXII., fol. CLIV–
CLVI., xvii.

original. It would require his abnormal memory to recount the whole life history of Pius II, as this does, or rather the series of his political achievements, for the life-history of Æneas Silvius Piccolomini was not quite what S. Antonino would have been pleased to relate in full consistory. He tells of the enthusiasm that broke over Florence when the cry was raised at midnight: "We have as Sovereign Pontiff the Lord Æneas Pius." Then he traces his picture of an ideal Pope, holy, austere, learned, the patron of arts, letters and reform, and endeavours by detailing some of the past exploits of Pius to show their grounds for expecting the new Pontiff to "bring to maturity the blossom of their hopes." Then the note changes, and in tones of sonorous eloquence to which his easily flowing Latin so aptly lends itself, he urges him to inaugurate the Crusade, bids him gather into one the angry powers of Europe, turn their swelling forces from each other, and direct them against the common foe of Christendom that had just taken and desecrated the holy places of Constantinople. This really fine and manly speech,[40] which at its close soars into the dignified and solemn adjuring style which the 15th-century writers so frequently adopted, made a deep impression on this brilliant, but unstable Pope. Its peroration rang in

---

[40] Vespasiano who seems to have heard both speeches, says that the one to Callixtus was "worthy" but this "the most worthy of all he delivered." Bisticci, *Vite di Uomini Illustri del Secolo XV*, 25.

his ears his whole life long. Its echoes roused him throughout his Pontificate to the same chivalrous ideas and still drove him in the decrepitude of stricken health and languishing old age to be carried, indomitable, to Ancona, that he might bless in person the puny, inadequate fleet that all his eloquence, his statecraft, and his treasure could bring against the Turk.

Within a year from this impassioned harangue, Fra Antonino passed away from life; and his passing was witnessed in his own city by this same Pope whose elevation to "the solicitude of all the Churches" he had thus joyously acclaimed.

VI

His Social Labours

IN their letter to S. Antonino urging him to accept the Archbishopric, the Florentine Magistrates especially insisted, it will be remembered, on the fact that the new office would mean ampler opportunities of work. They knew their Prior of S. Marco when they thought thus to tempt him.

Just eight years before, he had inaugurated a charity in Florence, which her restless character had rendered necessary. On Cosimo's return to power in 1436, that prince determined this time to establish a dynasty in Florence. Now just as other tyrants sought to crush their foes by assassinations and judicial murders, he with crafty foresight chose a weapon more deadly and efficient. The ruin would be more certain, because the root and source of his rivals' power would be destroyed.

"He employed taxes," says a chronicler, "as other princes used daggers, to rid himself of his opponents." Just before that date, the aristocratic party of the Albizzi had replaced the older, arbitrary system of taxation by an arrangement called the "Catasto," by which each citizen under penalty of confiscation reported his annual income and was taxed on it at the rate of seven per cent.;

and this declaration was to be remade every three years. Cosimo overthrew this equitable form of taxation and substituted for it the more ancient and unjust assessment by the ruling body, graduated, not according to income, supposed or declared, but according to political opinions. The result was the financial ruin and beggary of the Anti-Mediceans.

S. Antonino, though Cosimo's close friend and living on his bounty, was moved by the distress of these families, too proudly born to beg in their own city and too ruinously taxed to do anything but starve in silence. He thought out a solution to their miseries. His remedy was explained to twelve citizens whom he summoned to S. Marco. Their names are happily known to us, and their trades no less, for they show the hold that S. Antonino even then possessed on the entire city. Amongst them were alike the political friends and enemies of the Medici, wealthy bankers, notaries, drapers, silk-mercers, a shearer and a boot-maker. Before these he laid his scheme. This was to divide Florence up into six districts, over each of which two of the twelve were to be appointed. It would be their duty to collect funds, to seek out cases deserving of help and to disburse the moneys in their own divisions. Especially were they to direct their attentions to those most needy and least likely to complain, the *poveri vergognosi*, the shame-faced poor. Their headquarters were to be in the little Church of S. Martino, their directors the Friars of S. Marco, their title the *Provveditori dei Poveri Vergognosi*; but the simple people knew them and call them even today the *Buonomini di S. Martino*, the good men of S. Martin.

Nothing was to lie outside the scope of their charity; doctor's bills, sick nurses, dowries for marriageable daughters, premiums for a lad's apprenticeship, the redemption of pawn-tickets, gifts of beds, clothing, food, and money, were part of their material aids; while visiting the sick, the consoling of the faint-hearted, the staunching of sorrow's wide-gaping wounds, the spiritual comfort of prayers, Masses, sacraments completed the architectonic chivalry of this organisation.

To show moreover his independence of all save charity, which is love—and God is love—S. Antonino added two further injunctions: (i.) that the moneys received from benefactors were never to be funded, but simply taken and spent, for it showed want of delicacy, he thought, to traffic with the alms of the faithful; (ii.) that no authority, civil or ecclesiastical, was ever to demand an account of the sums received or expended, nor to take upon itself the direction of the society. Both injunctions the Government of Florence has at times in its history endeavoured unsuccessfully to set aside; but the continuance of the charity for five hundred years on the lines laid down by S. Antonino and its failure whenever it has been amended are pragmatic proofs of the wisdom of the saintly Prior.

As Archbishop, S. Antonino had a more extended scope for labour and was not one to neglect the ever-widening field, the expanse of which seemed to grow greater before him as he toiled onwards to the sunset and the dawn. Hardly had a year passed in his episcopal office, when one of these recurring mediæval plagues attacked the city fiercely. The Saint has told us of the horrors of the visitation and how the Magistrates voted him sums of money for the relief of the stricken people, but he has not told us of his own heroic labours. Fortunately we possess accounts left by others[41] who watched the gentle old man, leading his mule round the city, up and down its twisting, scrambling streets, carrying in paniers to poor and sick and dying what might be of most need. Wine, bread, vegetables, medicines, and the incomparable Bread of Angels were thus constantly at hand to be given out to the people. No wonder then that they recalled on his behalf the perfect example of the Master, who had done all things well. Their memories went back to the old stories of that One Perfect Figure who walked in miracle-working mercy the lanes of Palestine.

When the plague had spent its force, there followed an earthquake, which broke down even the solidly built houses of those days. Moreover, the accompaniment of comets and meteors

---

[41] Société des Bollandistes, *Acta* Sanctorum, 319, n. xviii.; 320, n.e; Summar. pro Canonis: cap. 4, n. xxxiii.

suggested some preternatural influence bent
on ruining Florence. Again the Archbishop
went on his errands of love, helping by gift and
counsel, while to aid him came a band of young
men of the *Buonomini* of S. Martin. He further
composed a treatise on these strange phenomena, "according to the doctrine of Aristotle and
Albertus Magnus," which for all its halting science was sufficient to root out of the hearts of
his flock their superstitious fear, instilled by the
weird happenings. S. Antonino was frightened
lest, if the plague came back, the fear occasioned
by the comets and other disturbances would
lay his people open to infection. For whatever
may be said about "faith-healing" can obviously be repeated even more emphatically about
"faith-destroying." Self-suggestion can certainly
cure, and no less certainly kill.

But there are as well in Florence even more
lasting monuments of his great episcopate in
permanent institutions set up for the betterment
of his flock. The *Spedale degli Innocenti*, famous
also for another reason, still cries out his name in
the streets. It was founded, it is true, long before
by Leonardo Bruni of Arezzo, the great literary glory of early Florentine Renaissance; but
it was not opened till 1444, when S. Antonino
took it under his especial protection. Children
had always charmed him, delicate child as he
himself had been, innocent as he remained till
he had passed "till where beyond these voices"
there is no more sin. Here, thought he, could be

established a useful institution for those hapless
little ones whom the dissolution of the bonds of
moral life was fast hurrying into the world. It was
to house and tend these born out of wedlock and
left to the public charge for their maintenance
that he converted the existing charity. So Lucca
and Andrea della Robbia made its walls alive
with their exquisite infant forms, the fascinating
beauty of which, made the more appealing by the
winsome gestures of outstretched hands, continuously calls upon the passerby for alms.

A similar enterprise, but one which shows
even more clearly the character of his work, is the
Bigallo. Originally begun by another Dominican
for another purpose, by S. Peter Martyr for a
military Order, the aim of which was to be the
forcible reduction of the anti-social *Paterini*, it
was turned by the good Archbishop to a gentler
use. The *Paterini* had all gone; perhaps because
the knights had seen to that, or perhaps because
the dependance on Rome, which Florence from
time to time found so necessary, made heresy
an unremunerative commercial investment. In
any case the *Paterini* had ceased to be of interest, and the knights had outlived their serviceableness. In fact the whole establishment had
somehow become merged in the famous Burial
Confraternity of the Brothers of Pity, whose
high-raised hoods of black, with the gruesome
eyeholes, at once revealing and concealing, may
be still noticed in Florence on their errands
of mercy. However, S. Antonino wanted an

orphanage for poor children. Here was a likely place, almost unoccupied. So he established in it an institution (though that hard-sounding phrase scarcely describes the smoothly moving home he set up) for the lost, vagabond, orphaned boys and girls of Florence.

His passion then was for the poor. All he had was at their disposal, for, Archbishop though he was, he was still bound by his vows as a Dominican Friar, whereby he was wedded to poverty. His time was laid out for their employment; his eloquence pleaded for them in the councils of the citizens; his pen championed their cause amid the graver gatherings of moral theologians; his memory hunted through the long-winding corridors of its astonishing retentiveness for texts from Sacred Scripture, the writings of the Fathers, the Decretals of the Popes, wherewith to assail the vulgar worship of wealth; his will broke through the crusted traditions of a hundred years and put on the vesture of liberality—a virtue his treatises unfalteringly extol. Perhaps to our modern ideas of things beautiful and becoming (and even it may be to his own generation which could be wooed and gladdened by the gay, delicious fruits and flowers of the exquisite Della Robbia) he went to excess, for he pulled up the garden which backed upon the episcopal palace, scattered its lovely blossoms, and drove the spade through the soft-grassed lawns of its Cathedral close. Here he planted a host of vegetables, chiefly cabbages and turnips, for his fond-loved poor; and in it for the most destitute he parcelled out allotments.[42]

After all this detailed work for God's wealth-less children, S. Antonino could still know that there were limits even to charity. It is necessary to make this reservation in these days, for the old spirit of what is called familiarly "indiscriminate alms-giving" has, alas, quite gone out of fashion. Our charities now are all organised. A strange thing, surely, to try to organize love! Only an unhumorous age could venture on such a para-dox. Still in deference to this modern spirit, it is only fair to S. Antonino to explain that he could detect and punish the impostor. Even the quaint picture of mediæval life that the following story reveals, makes it worth the telling.

A citizen of Florence had come to our Saint for a marriage-dowry for his three daughters. At his wits' end to raise any further sums, the Archbishop bade him hasten to the Church of the Annunziata and there beseech the Mother of all Mercy to hear his request. As in the fervour of his prayer he knelt in silence, the distracted father overheard two blind beggars, who, imag-ining themselves to be alone, were discussing their takings. They were in high feather over their success. One had got 250 gold crowns sewed into his cap, while the other had, hidden away on his person, 300 more. Back came the

---

[42] Société des Bollandistes, *Acta Sanctorum*; Process Canonis. Test. 46, 345.

citizen to the Saint to tell the conversation he had by chance overheard. Bitterly he denounced this abuse of public generosity, in proof of which he had brought with him the cap of the one and the cloak of the other. The Archbishop sternly reprimanded the two, not for begging for alms, but because they had begged when they had no need. As flagrantly as the wealth-loving merchants whom he so pitilessly denounced, they had broken his great law of contentment. Then with their consent, says the Chronicler,[43] he took their money from them, giving back to the one 25 ducats and 30 to the other. The rest he handed over for the dowries of the three girls. But not simply thus does the story finish. S. Antonino was not one to deal so hardly with the two blind men. The tale continues that "he charged himself with the maintenance of these beggars until the end of their lives."

Full of that charity that never falleth away, he took upon himself the whole administration of his own charities. Whenever he saw distress or could detect the hollow eye of want, there he was anxious to relieve by every means in his power. Where institutions were needed, or should be diverted to more pressing purposes, or were stranded for lack of funds, there he found scope for more extended and ampler labour. When famine or plague or earthquake had cast the shadow of death along the sunlit streets of

---

[43] Société des Bollandistes, *Acta Sanctorum*, 344.

Florence, he found his time elastic enough to allow him in person, not merely to organise but to oversee. Even individual cases of starvation or outcrying want were not too minute or too burdensome to be left to others to investigate. Only some young men of the city do we hear of as his helpers or the *Buonomini* or his own friars from S. Marco and S. Maria Novella. His household was reduced to six, but his ideals grew the grander; and his alms seemed like persistent streams from never-failing springs of wealth.

Yet was his charity ever true, rooted in faith and glowing with trustfulness in the inherent goodness of redeemed humanity. It was synonymous with justice, for it rested on fellowship and its piers were driven deep down into that human nature whereby all we mortals are akin. Charity for him was love, and God was love. Where then he found "storm and pestilence and famine and the waywardness of folk," there all the more were opportunities opening to him for showing his love of God through the unmistakeable working of his love for men.

VII

His Social Ideals[44]

UT S. Antonino was no mere doer of good deeds, without troubling himself any further as to their result. He worked out a very detailed and practical scheme of social advancement, which is alive with the same problems that harass the minds of our generation, and he even spelt it out in terminology that has about it the air of modernity. It is inevitable indeed that he should have been enormously influenced by the theories of Aristotle, who in those ages was regarded in the phrase of Dante, as the "Master of those that know." But his was no blind obedience, no dull following of another's ideas. To anyone who is familiar alike with the old classic writers and their more recent rivals, in social and political economy, the works of our Saint have a startling value, for they stand midway between and link together old and new. Even is there much to learn from the very fact that his circumstances were so very different from our own, his modes of thought and ours "as the poles asunder." They come upon us in a more startling way, stimulating us, widening our outlook beyond

---

[44] In this chapter plentiful use has been made of the volume by Carl Ilgner.

our own narrow furrow. Thus to look back trains the instinct for the path ahead; for to eyes not blinded "all the past, read true, is prophecy."

We must begin, says S. Antonino, at the beginning, we must first define what we mean by a "good thing." Here in this definition lies, he would suggest, the dividing line of all economic treatises. As a confirmed scholastic, then, he starts with a broad truth: "A good thing is what all desire." But he makes haste at once to qualify this remark before it has had time to work mischief. "'A good thing is what all desire," but God alone is absolute goodness, He alone is or can be desired for His own sake. All things else are desired in as much as they lead on to Him or are considered to lead on to Him. He can be sought for as an end, direct, pointing no further; but other things are but the objects of our desire because we conceive of them as taking us along the pathway of our pleasure, easing our steps in life's moving pursuit, guiding our journey in its onward march. He is the be-all and end-all; they are never to be the ultimate end of their own acquisition. The rest can boast themselves, in the highest meaning of the word, "useful" to human kind; but He lifts Himself up amid the other tumultuous purposes of existence and proclaims His incommunicable attribute of Finality.

It is then, S. Antonino would say, the first principle of economic science to recognise that riches are not intended as an end in themselves, but as a means to an end. When therefore a man begins to lay stress on the mere accumulation, the continual piling up, of wealth, without considering the power, or comfort, or security to be derived from it, he has obviously misunderstood the very purpose of trade. "God gave us natural riches (as property, cattle, food, and such like) and also artificial riches (as precious metals, clothing, etc.), so that we might by the application of them merit eternal life";[45] "God has bestowed wealth on man so that he might look on Him as the Well-wisher of the race, might love Him, and in His Name give alms to those in need";[46] "Temporal goods are given to us to be used in the preservation of our lives";[47] Hence he adds, "Production is on account of man, not man of production."

Riches then (i.e., the full complement of economic instruments) are good things, for on them the Father looked from the beginning with expressed pleasure. Hence whatever S. Jerome and his learned followers may note on the meaning of the word "Mammon" (viz., that it signifies in Syriac "iniquity") may be passed over as not of present interest. Wealth of whatever kind is good, if its usefulness be only properly apprehended. For all these things were ordained by God for the service of man.[48]

S. Antonino then will have none of that modern comfort which the millionaire preaches to

---

[45] Antonino, *Summa Theologica* Moralis, vol. 1. 7, 3, 533.
[46] Ibid., vol. 2, 1, 12, i., 192.
[47] Antonino, *Summa Theologica Moralis*, vol. 4, 5, 17, i., 254.
[48] Ibid., vol. 1, 13, 2, ix., 668.

the destitute, that poverty in itself is good. In itself, he says, it is an evil, though indeed out of it good may be obtained.[49] By his possessions man was intended to ward off the anxiety of the morrow and rest in simple content. He was to find in them his sustenance and livelihood, and to employ them in the support of his family. Beyond this immediate serviceableness the instruments of wealth, as has been observed already, have a nobler use in leading men on to God. For this removal of anxiety and this content are but the necessary conditions for man to have time and leisure to hold converse with His Maker. Moreover because in man the soul is of greater import than the body and has always the prior claims to allegiance, it follows that the whole science of economics (i.e., the science that seeks to regulate and adjust the relations between riches and life) is ultimately a moral one, and must be dominated by principles of justice and must harmonise with the Ten Commandments. Sin accordingly becomes an economic evil, and an economic evil in its completer sense becomes a sin.

It is possible therefore for these "goods" (wealth in its varied forms) to be turned to evil use; and this is because either they are evilly acquired or evilly distributed or evilly consumed.[50] Here S. Antonino forestalls the great modern division

---

[49] Ibid., vol. 4, 12, 3, 622.
[50] Ibid., vol. 1, 1, 12, I, 192; IV. 14, 2, 4, 735.

of Economics into Production, Distribution, and Consumption. It will therefore be more convenient and certainly clearer, to group the Saint's teaching under these three chief headings, instead of following his own order.

Production, says the Archbishop, is the law of life.[51] Other animals achieve their end through the blind operation of instinct; but man is called upon to accomplish his under the guiding compass of his reason. He must see to do his work, for work he must. It is his duty, his perfection and his happiness.

This labour is of various kinds, for the arts and crafts which man has devised are numberless. The staple trades of Florence are all passed in review;[52] the manufacture of wool, the associated building-trades, the working of metals, the shipping industry, agricultural production, pastoral cultivation of flocks and herds, the farming of fish and fowl, the medical profession and the stage are the special forms of man's "mechanical" skill which he instances by name. These are the chief means for the production of wealth.

Previous to the Fall (and the same still holds good with a not inconsiderable portion of mankind), manual labour was undertaken for no mere need, but for the pleasurable stimulus it gave the mind in exploring the powers of nature. But after the expulsion from Paradise it became

---

[51] Ibid., vol. 2, 8, 1, 291–293.
[52] Ibid., vol. 1, 1, 3, iii., 34.

for the majority of men a stern necessity, for the direct purpose of production is the sustaining of human life (our own or another's): "The object of gain is that by its means man may provide for himself and others according to their state. The object of providing for himself and others is that they may be able to live virtuously. The object of virtuous life is the attainment of everlasting glory."[53] Our modern haste and consequent over-production therefore would be repellent to him: "To acquire by labour the amount of food sufficient for preserving one's being requires only a moderate amount of time and a moderate amount of anxiety."[54]

But each man has his own peculiar bent or inclination, with which he has been endowed by Divine Providence for the more perfect harmony of the Universe. This proper, individual talent must be employed steadfastly by the possessor of it. The several members of the body natural, that by their diverse powers establish the just balance of a living organism, are paralleled by these varied tastes and occupations of the several members of the body politic. By this classic analogy, which is as old and as recent as political speculation, S. Antonino constantly finds help in his exposition of the social law.

Further it is well to notice that every work should be rightfully intentioned, be itself a lawful thing, and its achievement be executed with

---

[53] Antonino, *Summa Theologica Moralis*, vol. 1, 1, 3, iii., 34.
[54] Ibid., vol. 4, 12, 3, i., 623.

perfect prudence. Hence the Archbishop notes many of the faulty commercial practices of his day. It is as a Father Confessor that he is writing, treating economic science from the ethical point of view. He enumerates among other things false weights and measures, cloth not properly shrunk or so tightly stretched as to split at the slightest pressure put on it, houses built so badly that the roofs let in the wet and the walls were no protection against heat or cold, ill-seasoned wood for carving, paper that made all attempts at drawing on it a failure, ink watered beyond all usefulness, books badly bound or wretchedly coloured or filled out to an extravagant price by too wide margins and spaces.

Now this labour of man becomes partly complicated and partly simplified when the difference of the earth's productive force and the varied tastes and callings of individual men are taken into consideration; for it not infrequently falls out that one has a superfluity of some article of necessity, and a dearth of another, either because he finds the production of that one article more congenial to his nature or because his locality supplies it and not that other thing.[55] Hence came into existence commerce in its primitive form of barter; and, because barter was at times cumbersome and difficult of adjustment, money was invented as a medium of exchange. Then as forms of transit grew more rapid and international relations sped apace, the

---

[55] Ibid., vol. 3, 8, 1, 294–296.

ever-widening communications of commerce knit together all the world. It hastened from shore to shore, bringing peace in its wake, and giving to the whole commonwealth of man the particular benefits of each group of peoples.[56] With commerce too, truthfulness, justice and the other virtues assumed a new importance for their necessity became social as well as moral. Moral and social life were at once fused beyond all disentanglement: "Among men no social life is at all possible, except on the understanding that each speaks the truth. Therefore deceit, lying, and falsehood are destructive of human society, and truth its preserver."[57]

Along with all this, S. Antonino insists on the principle rightly understood, which Karl Marx has in recent years made so popular, that the value of things commercial (i.e., exchangeable) depends upon labour, whether of head or hand. Things in themselves are useless, until they have been either completed by human industry or at any rate transferred to more profitable markets by human labour.[58]

Now the question which in the Thirteenth, Fourteenth and Fifteenth Centuries agitated the intelligences of moralists was as to whether any gain in business was at all lawful and if so, up to what precise amount. This difficulty was part of a larger one, which dealt with the whole subject

---

[56] Antonino, *Summa Theologica Moralis*, vol. 1, 3, 3, 34–35; II., 1, 16, 3, 255.

[57] Ibid., vol. 4, 5, 15, iii., 247.

[58] Ibid., vol. 2, 1, 7, xvi., 99.

of usury. Starting from the principle of Aristotle that money cannot of itself beget money (phrased so admirably by Shakespeare in the paradox to "breed from barren metal") the mediæval writers were evidently puzzled as to how to justify the taking of interest. Money can be multiplied only by the labour of him to whom it has been lent out; consequently for the lender to make capital out of the very industry and commercial skill of the borrower was, in their opinion, opposed to the law of nature, for no man has any right to sell his own native capacity,[59] for by usury a man sells a thing twice over. "Money of itself does not increase, but becomes profitable in trade only by the skill of the trader."[60] "If the object of the trader is principally cupidity, which is the root of all evils, then certainly trade itself is evil. But that trade (as natural and necessary for the needs of human life) is, according to Aristotle, in itself praiseworthy, which serves some good purpose, i.e. supplying the needs of human life. If therefore the trader seeks a moderate profit for the purpose of providing for himself and family according to the becoming fortunes of their state of life, or to enable him to aid the poor more generously, or even goes into commerce for the sake of the common good (lest, for example, the State should be without what its life requires), and consequently seeks a profit not as an ultimate end but merely as a wage of

---

[59] Ibid., vol. 3, 1, 6, i., 70.
[60] Ibid., vol. 2, 1, 7, xvi., 99.

labour, he cannot in that case be condemned."[61]
S. Antonino goes on to take the case where a
man needs something, the loss of which will be
grave inconvenience to the owner. The latter may
in these circumstances demand a higher price,
not looking to the value of the thing in itself, but
its value to him, *i.e.*, not looking to the thing, but
to the inconvenience its loss will occasion him.
"I believe that any one can claim compensation,
not merely for the harm done him, but also for
the gain he might otherwise have obtained, if he
be a merchant accustomed to engage his money
in business. The same holds good, even if he be
not a merchant but have only the intention of
investing his funds in lawful trade; but not if he
be a man who hoards his wealth in coffers."[62] The
Archbishop is even at pains to justify the taking
of a percentage on bills of exchange, because of
their great convenience for travellers and pilgrims who would otherwise have to carry large
sums of money about with them.[63]

His argument all the way through is that
money is of itself not productive, but that its
profit comes from the skill, industry, energy of
the man who makes use of it. Therefore if one
man lends another money and expects a larger
return than the capital lent, it can only be
because of the industry, etc., of the man to whom
the money is lent. In other words the lender is

---

[61] Ibid., vol. 2, 1, 16, ii., 250

[62] Ibid., vol. 2, 1, 7, xviii., 101.

[63] Antonino, *Summa Theologica Moralis*, vol. 2, I, 7, xlviii.,
123.

taxing not his loan, but the personal qualities of the borrower, he is taxing what does not belong to him at all. Hence, in the eyes of the Saint, the only legitimate claim for interest could be that the lender was sacrificing a gain that he would otherwise have made in trade. Of course it is just this claim that nowadays holds good. According to our way of looking at it, the lender says to the borrower, "Yes, you can have my money, if you are willing to pay me for the use of it. I could get a percentage of profit in business with my capital, and if you want to induce me to put money into your concern, you must let me see that I do not lose by it."

The result of these quotations can, I think, be briefly stated by saying that S. Antonino denied the productivity of coin, but admitted the productivity of capital. So long as commerce dealt with a question of mere gold or precious metal, it was sheer usury to demand for its use an added sum called interest; but when funded accounts could be employed as capital[64] and become

---

[64] It can be established that S. Antonino had a clear idea of what we mean by *capital*, from the fact that he includes in the nature of a trade, not the mere material but the instruments as well; not only the water and fish, but the boats and nets. Even the very word is in his vocabulary: "*Pecunia in mercationibus ut vero capitali*" (Ibid., vol. 2, i. 7. xv. p. 99); and in another place, speaking of stock which through a period of over-production brings in no gain, he refers to "*amittant de capitali*" (Ibid., vol. 2, i. 8. iii., 129); and again still more clearly, "*Pecunia nisi per modum capitalis, ita ut emptionibus et mercationibus deputetur, not valet seipsum multiplicare (*Ibid., vol. 2, i., 8. xvi., 139*)*

distinct from passing currency, some form of interest was evidently lawful, for then came into play the loss sustained by the lender who might have put out his money into other commercial enterprises.[65]

Moreover there already existed State loans, which in Genoa, Venice, Florence, etc., paid to the citizens from whom the money had been borrowed an annual return which was regarded as a percentage on sums received. But these S. Antonino judges, on the authority of Master Nicholas, an English Dominican, to be allowable, for they were forced loans, exceedingly inconvenient, for which therefore the interest paid might be looked upon rather as compensation: "When there is any necessity, the State can demand from its subjects (even against their will) lawful help in money and personal service."[66] But forced loans disturb political security, so he begs the Civil Authority to come quite frankly and get the money it requires from its subjects, freely. To do this it must offer a percentage of interest to induce them to part with money that would otherwise be employed in trade, and this freely offered interest removes from the transaction all charge of usury. "When a prince allows usury, it is because he has in mind the good of his whole people, for there would be a great deal of harm done if there were

---

[65] Ibid., vol. 2, I, 11, ii., 163.
[66] Ibid., vol. 2, 11, 161–191.

no money that could be borrowed. And few would offer to lend money, unless they could get some profit by it."[67]

In a word, the principle that he advocates perpetually is that it is wrong to lend money directly for interest or to demand interest precisely as such. The intention may spoil the moral worth of the action. So long as the banker is prepared to demand a larger return for the moneys he has advanced to the merchant, solely on the ground of his loss, or the danger of his not getting repayment,[68] or of any other such reason he may be allowed to continue; but if his motive is simply to exact interest on the score of a loan, then he is a usurer and as such stands condemned. Hence he bitterly denounces "those of the nobility who are unwilling to work, and yet who directly seek by lending their money to merchants to secure an annual interest besides the eventual return of an undiminished capital," for he notices that though they call this "a deposit, it is clear usury."[69]

Having in this way settled that some gain is lawful in commerce, he endeavours to fix its amount, and ventures into the deep sea of maximum and minimum price. The value of an article, he here considers not in itself (*valor naturalis*), but precisely in relation to society (*valor usualis*), for though, he says, a mouse of itself

---

[67] Antonino, *Summa Theologica Moralis*, vol. 3, 3, 4, vii., 192.

[68] Ibid., vol. 3, 8, 3, i. p. 303; II. I, 7, xxi., 102.

[69] Ibid., vol. 2, I, 6, xx., 80.

as a living thing is of a higher value than dead wheat, yet to us men it is of much less value.[70] In this latter sense the value of an article depends chiefly on (i.) its usefulness, (ii.) its rarity or the difficulty of obtaining it, (iii.) its pleasurableness. Thus wheat bread is more valuable because more efficient than barley bread; corn more valuable in time of want than at other times because more rare; one horse or ornament more valuable to an individual because more productive to him of personal delight. Of course this last division rests on* the varying and reversible judgments of the particular tastes and fancies of individual men.

It is possible then for a prudent man to appraise the value of anything, not indeed with absolute exactness, but conjecturally and allowing for divergences of place and time and people. Indeed S. Antonino, following what he tells us was the legal practice of his century, allows half as much again of the appraised value as the maximum of selling-price, and half as little as the minimum of buying-price.[71] An article therefore that has been conjecturally valued at one florin could be conscientiously sold at any price up to one florin and a half, or conscientiously bought at any price down to half a florin. But these are the extreme limits.

Finally under the heading of production and the fixing of a just price, it is well to notice that

---

[70] Ibid., vol. 2, 1, 16, iii., 255–257
[71] Ibid., vol. 2, 1, 16, iii., 256.

S. Antonino fiercely forbids any formation of trusts or cartels or the authorizing of monopolies for the purpose of securing dearer prices. Above all, no power is to be allowed to individuals by the State of exploiting for their own ends the food and other necessaries of the people. When a man, he says, buys corn at harvest time and wine during the vintage so as to sell later at a higher price, Canon Law holds the profit obtained by this means to be unwarrantable, if it be done out of a lust for gain, but not if it be done out of necessity. This necessity may be private or public: public as in the case of Joseph who from foresight bought during the seven years of plenty to prepare for the seven years of want; private as when a man sees he will have nothing to sell later unless he buys immediately. He may in this case sell more dearly, but not above market price. But, "When monopolist merchants agree together to preserve a fixed price, so as to secure an unlimited profit, they are guilty of sinful trading." One canonist had suggested that the Bishop of the locality should declare authoritatively the limit of such profit. But S. Antonino, though equally desirous of some definite decision in particular cases would "rather take it out of the hands of the prelates and leave it to the Civil Authority, especially in fixing the price of food-stuffs and other things necessary to the people's life."[72]

---

[72] Antonino, *Summa Theologica Moralis*, vol. 3, 8, 3, iv., p. 306; II. 1, 16, ii., 252.

The Distribution of these "goods" in the community is no less a question of moral law, for it must be in strict accord with justice; else there will be continual turmoil in the State, restless constitution-making, unceasing friction between jarring factions each in turn exiling the other.[73] The good Archbishop of Florence had not to go far afield to learn all this. The uneven distribution of wealth, before and after the revolt of the *Ciompi* (disenfranchised) in 1396, was the cause of very many disturbances in his own city. Not indeed that S. Antonino desired an equal division of all property of the State, for it was the varied relationships of rich and poor, of ruler and ruled, which to his mind made up the harmony of the Universe: "Riches are not equally distributed. But this comes not by man's intention, for we often see that the most industrious are the least successful and the most idle abound in good things; nor is it due to the domination of some evil spirit acting without the Divine permission. But from the Lord God, either by direct ordinance or at least by His allowing it, comes this unequal distribution of wealth."[74] From the analogy of nature he argued against any dead level of exact humanity. For the intelligence of some is fit only to be under the direction of others; and the weakened wills of some need the supreme control of others; and the advancement of social well-being seems

---

[73] Ibid., vol. 3, 5, 3, v., 183–184.
[74] Ibid., vol. 2, 1, 12, i., 192.

only possible when the few govern the many.[75] Of course he has no intention of suggesting, as Aristotle would appear to have taught, that servants and masters were of a different human species, for God did not create "the poor from earth and the nobles from precious metals, but all we are descended from our father Adam, of whom it is written that God made him from the dust."[76] So that S. Antonino steadfastly holds to it that the inequality of possessions and power in the world is due to Divine permission or even to a direct Divine command; it stands as an utterly irremediable law.

But it does not follow from this that the present state of society is such as God would have it to be. For first of all the Archbishop lays it down as an indisputable principle that it is the duty of the State to provide for all its members.[77] Even when they have got past work, or for some other reason (such as ill-health, etc.) are unable to support themselves, then society has the right and the duty to take from those who have more than they need and to hand it over to their less fortunate fellow citizens: "For whosoever sustenance his own labour sufficeth not, the others of his own society who can work harder than they have need or who possess riches, are obliged to provide by the natural law

---

[75] Ibid.
[76] Ibid., vol. 2, 4, 4, vi., 581.
[77] Ibid., vol. 2, 1, 11, i., 161.

of charity and friendship."[78] Poverty therefore in the sense of destitution must be ruled out of the State.[79] Everyone should have a sufficiency of food, clothing, and accommodation and, unless such is guaranteed to the subjects, the rulers are at fault: "For this reason has God established the rich and mighty over the poorer folk that they should provide, not for their own private ends, but rather for the common good."[80] "The prince ought diligently to see to it that there be no want in the city, but rather abundance of provisions. For this reason he must foresee and prevent any such destitution, by providing especially for the corn of the people."[81] "It is to the interest of the State to concern itself with the citizens, that they be not dragged down into poverty."[82] From whatever cause then the people are in distress, whether through their own fault or not (for S. Antonino makes no distinction at all), the State is bound to provide, though it may inflict punishment at the same time upon all who will not work according to their ability. Upon all lies what one may call the great law of content; the duty of working for one's own support and acquiring a sufficiency or "decency" over and above the necessaries of life. This duty is of moral obligation, for, says the Archbishop

[78] Antonino, *Summa Thologica Moralis*, vol. 4, 12, 3, i., 623.
[79] Ibid., vol. 2, 1, 11, i., 161.
[80] Ibid., vol. 4, 3, 6, ii., 86.
[81] Ibid., vol. 3, 3, 1, v., 170; IV., 2, 6, i., 64.
[82] Ibid., vol. 2, 11, 1, i., 161.

with something of that fire with which Rousseau set the Revolution ablaze, "the good of the State is something divine."[83]

Thus we may say the Saint looked far ahead. He views social life with friendly feeling. The family, with its triple group of relationship between master and servant, man and wife, parent and child, is "the union of domestic persons through daily actions ordained to the necessities of life."[84] In it the wife's position is "to be solicitous and anxious over what is done in and for the family, and therefore to remain at home."[85] She is not to take upon herself the offices of her husband whose business it is to engage in trade lest the family be without the means of subsistence. And though he has gentle scorn for those who glory in their equipages as if "God was foolish in giving men legs at all,"[86] he is human enough in feeling to allow women to wear false hair "if their station demands it or if thereby they are more pleasing to their husbands."[87] "God inspires the minds of men to furnish hospitals in which provision shall be made for the poor and destitute, for healthy as well as for sick, and for foundlings."[88] He speaks also of homes for the aged, for wayfarers, for orphans, for quite small babies,

---

[83] Ibid., vol. 4, 3, 6, 86.
[84] Ibid., vol. 1, 14, 6, v., 757.
[85] Ibid., vol. 4, 2, 5, ii., 55.
[86] Ibid., vol. 2, 4, 4, vi., 581.
[87] Ibid., vol. 2, I, 23, xiii., 326.
[88] Ibid., vol. 3, 11, i., 482.

and warns the attendants to persevere in their charitable efforts even if the inmates be ungrateful and discontented. He alludes also (it is said, a rare thing in the Middle Ages) to hospitals set apart solely for the sick.

When such institutions are rich the doctors should be well-paid, for they are to help the patients not with medicines only but with kindly words, and these, it is hinted, are not likely to come from a discontented man.[89] Evidently too the idea is contemplated of doctors salaried by the State (*medici salarati a communitate*[90]). And it is interesting to note that when discussing the administration of hospitals, S. Antonino considers that women should certainly direct such as are for women only, and even in such as are for men, he sees nothing incongruous in women nurses and matrons.[91] A last quotation may be allowed to speak for itself and is typical of the author: "Chemists sin when selling unnecessarily on holidays of obligation, but of course there is no sin when medicines are sold for the sick or when such like transactions take place; for as regards this, in all well-regulated cities like Florence, the laws arrange that each chemist's shop successively shall be open for a short time, so that, at any hour of the day, there will always be one to which the people can go."[92]

---

[89] Ibid., vol. 3, 10, I, i., 483.
[90] Ibid., vol. 3, 7, 2, 283.
[91] Antonino, *Summa Thologica Moralis*, vol. 3, 11, 482–503.
[92] Ibid., vol. 3, 8, 4, vi., 318.

As a young man he had seen visions, as an old man he dreams dreams. He sketches out in terms curt and philosophic, without one trace of rhetoric or declamation, a city wherein the poor and sick shall be provided for in hospitals[93] and institutions;[94] where property shall be more fairly distributed; where family-life made up of complementary beings, the husband and wife, whose work and genius are the more peaceably united because so totally distinct, shall be the centre of the State's preoccupation;[95] where the children shall be properly educated in the knowledge of God, in letters, and in the arts and crafts useful to them in acquiring their livelihoods.[96] Here masters and servants with their mutual duties of forbearance, personal supervision, and just remuneration on the one hand, and of obedience and honest labour on the other[97] shall unite in perfect peace. Here the individual right to acquire private property shall be absolutely recognised as of Divine natural law, but the exercise of that right be restrained by direction of the State, which may even, should need arise, insist on the common ownership by the State of all the forms of wealth. Still it is only fair to the State to note that he regards such a state of society as violent and impracticable but not evidently contrary to

---

[93] Ibid., vol. 4, 3, 6, ii., 86.

[94] Ibid., vol. 3, 3, 6, ii., 196.

[95] Ibid., vol. 4, 2, 5, ii., 56–57; I. 14, 5, iv., 735.

[96] Ibid., vol. 4, 2, 6, i., 64.

[97] Ibid., vol. 4, 2, 5, vi., 60; IV, 2, 5, vii., 61–62.

justice.[98] Finally his most trenchant sayings concern the just wage which every worker should receive. This should be paid promptly and be according to the condition of the labourer, his skill, the danger of his occupation, the need and number of his children, the customs of the country, etc.[99]

Lastly as a sign of S. Antonino's gentle tenderness, a short sentence may be quoted wherein he lays it down that an employer of labour should "rather care for and tend his sick workmen than be in a hurry to send them away into a hospital."[100]

The last great division of political economy concerns Consumption. Here also, as we have before quoted from S. Antonino, evils may come in. For it is a sad thing to see, side by side, extravagance and penury, to see horses and mules gaily caparisoned while the poor perish from hunger; or in a plague-stricken city when the sick lie naked, cold, and foodless to find men and women dressed with vain and gaudy ornaments.[101] Extravagance is as much a social and moral evil as the unjust distribution of wealth. Each person has a prime obligation to support himself and his family. When this has been discharged he has the further duty of paying to the society to which he belongs its lawful taxes, such as the rulers are

---

[98] Ibid., vol. 2, 1, 14, i., 224–225.
[99] Ibid., vol. 3, 8, 4, 308; II, 1, 17, viii., 268–269.
[100] Ibid., vol. 3, 3, 6, vii., 201.
[101] Ibid., vol. 2, 4, 4, vi., 581; II. 4, 5, ii., 591.

obliged to impose for the proper administration of their dominions, for the security of the roads,[102] for the safe-guarding against times of famine,[103] for the beautifying of the city,[104] etc. These taxes the citizen is, for social reasons, morally obliged to pay; and by making a false declaration of income (is S. Antonino thinking of the *catasto?*), a man commits theft against the State and is bound to restitution—unless of course it is a generally recognised custom for each to give in an incomplete balance-sheet. On the other hand taxation indulged in out of class-hatred or political spite is no less unjust. The citizens so acting commit mortal sin and are bound to restitution.[105]

After his duties of justice to himself, his family, and his State, (it is on this order that the Saint lays great stress), the citizen is bound to almsgiving, according to his means. From his superfluities he must dispense to the needy and poor and to the adornment of God's temples. But this obligation is rather of charity than of justice, so that before he gives to beggars or the Church he must pay his debts. In this relation he quotes with evident approval a saying of S. Ambrose: "The Lord desireth not the pouring out of wealth, but its administration." The

---

[102] Antonino, *Summa Theologica Moralis*, vol. 2, 1, 12, vi., 195–196.

[103] Ibid., vol. 4, 2, 6, i., 64.

[104] Ibid., vol. 4, 3, 6, ii., 86.

[105] Ibid., vol. 2, 1, 13, iii., 215.

importance of this prudent distribution of alms is apparent, he says, from the point of view alike of rulers and subjects.[106] "It is not sufficient that a man give alms, he must also take the trouble to give them in the right way."[107] Hence he is careful to note that true generosity does not consist merely "in the suitable use and administration" of money, but it requires as well "the preparing of opportunities for its proper exercise."[108]

Last of all, over and beyond these obligations comes the virtue of magnificence or generosity. This is a virtue which evidently appealed enormously to our Saint, for it is inculcated in almost every chapter of his stupendous work. To Florentines especially, who loved their city with a passionate devotion and whose eyes were gladdened by things of beauty, reared by wealthy patriots to the honour of God or His Mother or Messer San Giovanni Battisto or to others of the Saints, and whose lives were lived amid all that was most noble in architecture, painting, sculpture, or letters, magnanimity was no vulgar display of unjustly earned wealth but an instinctive desire to leave their country the more splendid for their achievements.

These ideals of Florence set out in four volumes of S. Antonino's *Summa Moralis*, put into complete activity in the Greater and Lesser Guilds, and lined in stone along the graceful

---

[106] Ibid., vol. 4, 5, 3, v., 183.
[107] Ibid., vol. 2, 1, 24, iv., 336.
[108] Ibid., vol. 4, 5, 17, i., 253.

facade of Orsanmichele are commercial, it is true, but clean and religious and noble. They sum up a chivalrous and knightly aspect of mercantile adventure. They spell out the splendid Chronicles of the Romance of Trade.

VIII

His Other Literary Work

SOCIAL theories, however, were only one
portion of S. Antonino's literary work. Busy
as his life was, and full of manifold cares
and labours, he managed to leave behind him
no mean record of work accomplished. He had
been taught little at school, still he had learnt a
great deal for himself from books and more from
experience. His time however was seldom his
own. Hardly had he finished his noviciate, than
the burdens of office were laid on him and they
grew with the growth of each successive appointment. Priorships needed much of his attention,
his Vicariate over the Lombard Congregation
entailed "journeyings often," his superintend-
ing of the building of S. Marco meant further
inroads on those leisured moments. To all these
succeeded the overwhelming occupations of the
Archiepiscopate, with its religious and State
duties and its not infrequent embassies. It is
therefore with feelings of wonder that we look at
the long row of tomes that he has left us as monuments of "perpetual industry." To accomplish
them his energy was enormous, for his friend
Castiglione tells us that after Matins were over
(i.e., about 4 o'clock in the morning) until 9 a.m.,
the Saint was wont to read and write, study and

compose his works. To assist the labours of his
pen, he brought an astonishing memory. The feat
of his boyhood, learning by heart the crabbed
pages of the dull *Corpus Juris*, seems to have been
no isolated fact, but (although under the influence of God's designs for him) a result of natural endowment. The same gift, at any rate, was
conspicuous throughout his life. Parallel with
this was his persistent energy. There was no limit
to his labour; and as the frail boy, whose delicate
beauty had made his friends and superiors fear
an early decline,[109] grew to be venerable in years,
his intelligence also increased from strength to
strength.

But there is a particularly personal passage
in the Prologue of the *Summa Moralis* which
gives S. Antonino's idea of his own individual
genius. Even in a translation, it can be seen to
be a charming page of genuine literature. After
quoting the Scriptural tribute to the industry of
the ant (Prov. 6:6–8), he continues:

> And I betwixt the summer and autumn of my
> life, deem it necessary to gather up my har-
> vest of knowledge; lest when the winter of
> my age set in, I perish of hunger. For old age
> is fit for little work, so weary grows it in its
> labours, it stumbles with its halting memory
> and darkening sight, and has but little time to
> turn the pages of books. So already feeling the
> tediousness of things, I seek to shake it off by

---

[109] Société des Bollandistes, *Acta Sanctorum*, 319.

the example of the ant, tiny animal as it is, but wise beyond other's wisdom. For "having no captain or master" (Prov. 6:7), she provides for herself against the winter; so too I confess that I have had no master in grammar, except when I was a little boy—and he was a sorry teacher; nor in any other study except in dialectics and that was a very much interrupted course; nor again have I had any superior who has forced me to study, as I have been almost continually myself superior. Still eagerly drawn by the sweetness of truth, especially of the moral sciences, I have collected from among all my reading these few notes which have especially appealed to me. And just as the ant gathers up for its food, not what it considers most precious, but what best suits it; so I have given the go-by to all those higher problems and have set down only what I consider most apt for the purposes of preaching, hearing confessions and counselling souls, not as though composing some vast work, but rather giving the fruit of my experience to my best-loved friends whose genius lies not in metaphysics or whose books are few or whose time for reading is much broken up. ...

Stern is the travail of the ant in its struggle for life; no less stern, as I think, have been my labours throughout long years, interruptedly spent on other business, not of greater value, but more pressing. Thus it has been that sometimes for whole months and years together, I have not added one single stroke to this book, stealing from my occupations a few moments for taking food or for the exigencies of my office, which all-unworthy I have held so long, or for the befitting business of a religious, namely prayer and contemplation. [110]

These lines do really give a fair and correct view of S. Antonino's genius, his spirit of persistent labour. To this must be added his possession of an amazing clearness of expression. This does not indeed mean that the originality should be excluded from his gifts, for the book about which he speaks here with so much diffidence brought about a revolution in the ecclesiastical learning. He was the first author to separate ethical from dogmatic theology. The Fathers of the Church seem seldom to have concerned themselves with more than passing references to moral science. S. Ambrose has indeed a work on usury, but it purports to be a commentary on Tobias, just as S. Gregory's notes on Job were in the main didactic homilies. S. Augustine breaks through established precedents in composing a treatise on lying. This however was almost all that had been done. Then the earlier scholastics in their works treated of moral problems rather as parts of some doctrinal discussion in which they lay embedded. Teachers too of the type of Alexander of Hales and S. Thomas Aquinas

---

[110] Antonino, *Summa Theologica Moralis*, 3–4.

gathered together what they could find relating to the study of ethics, while Canonists like S. Raymund Peñafort ranged over all Christian literature to discover legal points settled by Popes or Councils or Bishops. But these writers treated morals as dependent either on dogma or on law. After them followed the mediæval lists of actual cases of conscience with the solutions to them arranged in alphabetical order but very incompletely prepared.

S. Antonino entered into their labours. The *Corpus Juris* and the *Summa Theologica* were the basis from which he worked. These he took severally to pieces and from their chosen materials built up a new science, the science of morals. His aim was to establish the great principles of moral action, and by their means help the conscience in its decisions of everyday life. For this faculty is a thing so delicate, so subject to environment, so susceptible of education, that experience of life, probity of character and prudence of judgment are gravely needed in the direction of it. All these S. Antonino possessed. To him came,[111] in all their difficulties, the citizens of Florence, merchants to consult him on the legitimacy of certain transactions, bankers on the limits of usury, guild-men on the exact amount of labour they were morally bound to contribute, mothers to ask his advice in their household toils and on the education of their children, priests to hear

---

[111] Société des Bollandistes, *Acta Sanctorum*, 321.

his interpretation of synodical decrees and papal pronouncements, rulers to question him on the lawfulness of taxation and the fitting adornment of the city. It was not so much that his knowledge was particularly extensive. There were certainly more learned men than he within the walls of Florence; but his prudence and impartiality of judgment, once a case was proposed to him, were of extraordinary value. Hence he got the name of Antonino the Counsellor;[112] and from his court, the Pope allowed no appeals to Rome.[113]

His method in the *Summa* is to give the ordinary view of moralists on the subject of the discussion. Where however there had been great divergence of opinion, he breaks off into an historical disquisition, citing passage after passage from the writings of previous canonists to show the growth of a particular attitude or the reason for no longer following some earlier authoritative decision. Then he gives his own view, or where he sees no necessity for that, he simply leaves the problem unsolved. If however, he comes to a definite decision, it is done in no arbitrary way; he gives all his reasons, answers objections, and then dispassionately goes on to the next point. It is noticeable, too, that he more usually inclines to the less severe side. But an exception to this gentleness of judgment must be made in the matter of justice, in which he

---

[112] Société des Bollandistes, *Acta Sanctorum*, 321.
[113] Ibid., 323; Moro, *Di S. Antonino*, 58.

is exceedingly rigorous. Any infringement of
another's right, any keeping back of another's
well-earned wage, any scamping of honest hard
work, any extortionate demand for usury comes
in for stern criticism. Very little injustice passes
unrebuked.

The passages from the Prologue which we
have quoted some pages back speak of this work
as very interruptedly composed, and as stretch-
ing over several years. It is interesting to see that
this statement is borne out by little local touches
scattered up and down these four volumes.
Towards the beginning of the Third Book[114] he
speaks of the year 1448; at the end of the same
volume[115] he has already advanced to 1449. Again
in the Fourth Book, we find reference to the year
1455;[116] and the last treatise can only have been
finished at the end of his long life.

To these four volumes of his *Summa Moralis*
must be added a fifth, which however in actual
fact was really written before the others. It is his
Chronicle or *Summa Historialis*, meant to round
off his study of ethics by a full plan of all Church
history. Somewhat disordered, to our more modern concept of historical literature, it is a vast
repertorium of biographical notices arranged
much on the same lines as those amazing
works of the Thirteenth Century, by Vincent de
Beauvais and others, in which every sort of fact

[114] Antonino, *Summa Theologica Moralis, Tit.* 6, *cap.* 3, 5.
[115] Ibid., 31, 2, 8
[116] Ibid., 8, 1, 4

is collected and recorded. Legends of the Saints, remarks on natural phenomena, legal decisions, theological discussions are thrown down into this sea of knowledge. The result is much more like an encyclopædia than an ordered history. The parts of it that deal with early history, though no doubt to S. Antonino they appeared to be of most importance, are to us of little value. He accepts more or less credulously whatever his predecessors bequeathed to him; in reality he could do little else, for he had none of that critical apparatus which enables us to sift out the true from the false. But when he comes down to his own time, much of his information is first-hand and valuable. He had seen a good deal of Italy, had mixed with the Papal Court, had sat in the Council of Florence and had mingled with the throng of various nationalities that met in the presence-chamber of Latin Pope and Grecian Patriarch. To Emperors both of East and West he had spoken, though he had but a poor opinion of either. As a friend of Cosimo he had opportunities of grasping the threads of European diplomacy; and through Fra Angelico must have seen at S. Marco's the artistic leaders of Florence at the greatest period of her history. Consequently his Chronicle as it nears his own day grows fuller and more interesting. It is enlivened occasionally by gossip, and, considering the formal manners of that time, is refreshingly free and independent. It is this mixture of facts in more or less disorder, half legendary and half critical, humorous and redolent of piety, that makes the volume one of the most fascinating of mediæval treatises. S. Antonino has none of the quaintness of Villani or the freshness of Morelli, but the evident desire on his part to tell the whole truth and his great wealth of anecdote make his book most pleasant reading.

The other works of the Saint consist of treatises on moral[117] questions, or else pious instructions for priests, or letters written to ladies[118] for the direction of their conscience. Some are in Latin, some in Italian, but it would be tedious to examine each in turn. They contain little that adds to our knowledge of his character, though here and there a fact may be gleaned from them. For instance in the *Conclusiones et Decisiones in foro Conscientiæ*, we find that these were written in answer to certain questions put by Dominic of Catalonia and were composed during the pontificate of Eugenius IV, when our Saint was not yet Archbishop. He excuses himself for the unfinished state of the notes by saying that they were scribbled off while he was at the Baths

---

[117] He composed also a catechism for children, printed in Venice 1493. It is the oldest, we are told, of all catechisms, taking the word in its strictest sense. See Otto Braunsberger, *Stimmen aus Maria Laach: Katholische Blätter* (Freiburg im Breisgau: Herder'sche Verlagshandlung, 1897), 174. It has been republished lately: Pietro Tacchi Venturi, *Storia della Compagna di Gesù in Italia*, vol. 1, Roma-Milano: Società Editrice Dante Alighieri, 1910), 277–281.

[118] e.g., his fascinating letter to Diodata degli Adimari on the death of her little boy; Antonino, *Lettere*, XV, 149–154.

during some time of illness and had no books at hand.

Into the great discussion, then beginning to rend all Christendom, as to the educational value of the Classics, S. Antonino does not deliberately enter. As a disciple of Fra Giovanni Dominici, his face had been set against all pagan authors; but he loved them too much himself to have the heart to exile them forever from life. His own devotion to Plato almost carried him away, for the fascination that author possessed for him was so great that he had to stop and read through Aquinas's *Summa contra Gentiles* (S. Thomas's defence of Christianity against paganism) before he dared continue the *Dialogues*.

With that marked prudence which stamps his every page, he thus sums up his own opinion of the ancient authors: "One has no right, simply because these poets and orators were men of vicious lives, to scorn whatever there is in their writings of truth and usefulness. Truth wherever found can be from the Holy Spirit of God alone, even if the teachers of it have not the same Spirit within their hearts by saving grace."[119]

As a critic, a moralist, an historian and a preacher, he had few gifts of eloquence. But his sympathy with all distress is so keen, and his judgment so sound and balanced in such perfect poise, that his every word is a word of wisdom.

---

[119] Antonino, *Conclusiones et Decisiones in Foro Conscientiae* (Venice: Petrus de Quarengis, 1497), vol. 1, 1, 4, iv., 37.

IX

His Character

NOW that the events of the life of S. Antonino have been set out, at least in some detail, it will be possible to consider the Saint himself. For although what he was is infinitely of more account both to himself and to us than what he did, we have no means of judging his character until we have first studied its outward expression in the works of head, hand, and heart. We must pass along the cloister, and up through the stately nave before we dare venture into the locked shrine and peer behind the veil.

Fortunately his biographers have given us passing glimpses of the man as they knew him; and there is also something to be found in the heaped-up miracles and acts of heroic sanctity which link up the long Process of Canonization. His appearance as a boy is repeatedly described, but without any definite details. A slight frail figure, rather delicate physique, an almost girlish beauty is the sole picture which these descriptions can call up. The later non-contemporary authors speak of his short stature, apparently basing their statements on the diminutive form "Antonino." But beyond the fact that he was not robust-looking, there is no evidence at all to prove him to have been undersized. As a matter of actual history, when the coffin was opened by Cardinal Alessandro de' Medici at nightfall on May 7th, 1589, the body was measured, and the sworn evidence of eyewitnesses reported by a Notary Public gives the length as "2⅚ Braccia,"[120] equal in English measurement to about 5 ft. 5 in.—quite average height. Moreover, as we have already suggested, the pet name of Antonino is perfectly explainable on grounds of affection and popularity.

It is interesting to read that when the Cardinal removed the lid of the coffin and gazed on the body that had laid undisturbed for one hundred and thirty years, he recognised the face from the accurate portraits that then existed in Florence and were well-known in the city. This is fortunate testimony, for we can be certain that the painting by Fra Bartolomeo, taken from the death-mask, and the terra-cotta bust, both at S. Marco's, represent faithfully the features of the Saint.[121]

His temperament seems to have been naturally phlegmatic. He hints as much himself, for he quotes with approval a passage from the works of Albertus Magnus in which that learned psychologist briefly notes how different branches of knowledge attract different characters: "The optimist takes to natural science,

---

[120] A braccio in Florence, for it differed considerably in each of the great Italian cities, was equal to .5836 of a metre.
[121] As for the much-discussed portrait of the Saint in the famous "Crucifixion" of Fra Angelico, see: Douglas, *Fra Angelico*, 89–90.

the pessimist to poetry, the hasty-tempered to mathematics and metaphysics, and the phlegmatic to the moral sciences," where he is evidently alluding to himself. But even apart from this, his biographers speak of his extraordinary composure of countenance which nothing could disturb.[122]

A story is told,[123] which exemplifies his calm manner even in rebuke. One day a citizen of Florence brought to the Archbishop a dish of apples. In gratitude the Saint made answer by invoking on him God's blessing—*Dio tel meriti*. The man evidently thought such pious talk to be a very inadequate reward and showed his feelings by leaving the palace with very disappointed looks. At once the Saint saw what was amiss and recalled his benefactor. Scales were sent for, and on a scrap of parchment were written the words of blessing. In the one balance were put the apples, in the other the scroll. Down went the paper, outweighing even the kindly gift of fruit. The gentle miracle taught lessons that no harsh reproof could have so speedily instilled. Even after all these years the parable has its use and meaning.

In his books, too, can be traced the same unemotional temperament, for, though enlivened by gleams of quiet humour, they are never written with any rhetorical or turgid appeals to sentiment. Moreover, partly by reason of his

---

[122] Ser-Uberti, "Notes," 330.
[123] Société des Bollandistes, *Acta Sanctorum*, 345.

stupendous memory and partly by reason of this same phlegmatic turn of mind, he was burdened with the desire of perpetual accuracy. At table, when the reading went on, no falsely pronounced word or quantity, no mistaken date ever passed uncorrected;[124] and in the ceremonies in Church and at the great State functions, he was never at fault, never broke any of the prescribed rubrics.[125] This should not convey the impression that he was at all pompous in his dealings with others: witness one of his letters: "When you write to me please leave out all recommendations and reverences and affections and say what you want, and I'll answer you without any preambles."[126]

This same even character it was that made him the best of counsellors in any trouble and the clearest disentangler of twisted difficulties. Nothing disturbed his judgment, nothing prejudiced him, nothing blinded him to the merits of any case. He became the embodiment of that most uncommon and therefore most terrifying of gifts, common sense. Whatever he took up, on whatever he pronounced judgment, the absolute balance of truth was clearly established. We may dread to meet such accurate and impartial conversationalists, because we are in the main so inaccurate and slipshod ourselves; but once encountered they are the most steadying and fascinating of companions.

---

[124] Société des Bollandistes, *Acta Sanctorum*, 321.
[125] Ibid., 323.
[126] Antonino, *Lettere*, XV, 154.

S. Antonino, with his piercing power of observing character, notes that such a temperament as his had many advantages, for it tends of its own nature to be patient and modest. And that he certainly was. But he also admits quite frankly that it brings with it other disadvantages, as for example a constitutional inclination towards laziness and negligence.[127] In the light of the psychological observation of S. Thomas Aquinas that it is just his weaknesses that a man of character strengthens, it is startling to see how this negligence and laziness, the seeds of which S. Antonino discovered in his own heart, were the very last imperfections to which strangers were at all likely to have supposed him subject. How persistent must have been the struggle by which the Saint became so admirable an example of untiring energy and painstaking thoroughness! He adds also that a man of his temperament was naturally peaceful and therefore not infrequently subject to fears. From his life such a weakness had been banished early. His books and sermons are astonishingly full of candour and fearlessness. He rebukes rich and poor, Cosimo and the Magistrates,[128] priests, merchants, rebels, whenever he thinks that blame ought to be laid by one in his pastoral office. We read also of how he fought the Signory or Government of the city, and forced them to obey the laws and respect the liberties of Florence. Especially do we find

---

[127] Antonino, *Summa Theologica Moralis*, vol. 1, 1, 6, i., 50.
[128] Moro, *Di S. Antonino*, 61.

him insisting on free and unhampered elections and on the correct counting of the white and black beans which were used in balloting.[129] On one occasion when they threatened to depose him from his Archbishopric, he smilingly pulled out from his pocket the key of his beloved cell in S. Marco, and told them he was only too anxious to be back in his old home. On another, he actually left his palace and went into the cloister, till Cosimo yielded and hurried off to bring him back.[130]

His energy moreover is written large in all his works. The *Summa Moralis* is an evident monument, composed as it was during many years of his life, in odd moments snatched from his official duties. The persistent continuance of such a labour under such difficulties is a remarkable tribute to industry. None but those who have tried to write in broken snatches of time, can tell how repulsive such toil becomes. On each occasion the thread has again to be taken up, the design of the work revised, the same tints and colours matched; else the result will bear more resemblance to a patchwork quilt than to clearly pictured tapestry. But it was not merely a question of interrupted labour, an added obstruction was that almost the only time he had for writing was in the early morning when his whole nature called out for rest. He worked late into the night.

---

[129] Bisticci, *Vite di Uomini Illustri del Secolo XV*, 21–22; Société des Bollandistes, *Acta Sanctorum*, 342.

[130] Société des Bollandistes, *Acta Sanctorum*, 344.

"I have no more paper or light, and Francis is calling for this, so I end" is the close of one of his letters;[131] and another shows his speed and crowded hours: "In haste, without rereading. I don't know if I have missed out any words."[132] Yet there he sat from 4 a.m. to 9 a.m., working at his sermons, his reading, and his books. Canon Castiglione often wondered how his Archbishop could keep up his enthusiasm for study and was puzzled to account for the wakeful hours of mental labour when his eyes must have been almost closing from sheer want of sleep. The marvel remained unsolved, save as a fiercely determined act of will. But from time to time sleep would triumph, and the Saint would turn his chair round and tilt it up against the wall, and in that boyish attitude get what refreshing sleep he could.[133]

Boyish indeed he always remained to the end, with all a boy's humour and a boy's gravity. His too was the boy's passionate purity, for he had "passed by the ambush of young days." His letters to his friends and relations, especially the one written to the Prior and friars of Pistoja on the death of his old novice-master, Bl. Lawrence of Rippafratta,[134] reveal his simplicity and candour, and his singular freshness of mind. One friend noted his "childlike soul"; another remarked that even till his death he remained "like a boy of fifteen."

---

[131] Antonino, *Lettere*, VIII, 116
[132] Ibid., XV, 154.
[133] Société des Bollandistes, *Acta Sanctorum*, 332.
[134] Antonino, *Lettere*, XXIV, 198–202.

His last great natural gift was the most blessed of God's prerogatives, the gift of making friends. His loveableness can be traced from the early days when the children with whom he played and the neighbours called him simply "little Antony." It shows when he climbed the hill of Fiesole and the Bl. Giovanni Dominici looking on him loved him. It knit him in bonds of an almost schoolboy friendship with Fra Angelico, whose eye for angelic loveliness could find in S. Antonino a human reflexion of what his soul had seen in its joyous wanderings through the realms of fancy. Then as the will of his brethren pushed him into offices of responsibility, we find him regarded with enthusiastic reverence. The younger friars looked up to him, captivated by his gentle kindness, and no less by the astonishing breadth of mind which his intelligence displayed; for nothing so charms young age as to find old age encouraging and tolerant. Nor was the love merely one-sided. Castiglione tells how he, who lived for eight years in S. Antonino's closest company, was cared for by the Archbishop with all the watchfulness of affection; he notes too how when Mark, the other of the Saint's devoted secretaries, died, S. Antonino, ageing and tremulous, completely broke down. "The staff of my life had failed me" was all that he could say.[135] Cosimo too despite many differences of ideas and ideals, kept his cell in S. Marco, opposite to the Archbishop's and used to come and stay for days and talk as

---

[135] Société des Bollandistes, *Acta Sanctorum*, 319.

only friends talk. Even Eugenius IV, hard, strong, and crafty, when he felt the approach of death[136] sent for his Archbishop of Florence that from his lips might come the absolving words, and from his hands the sealing of holy oil, and from his prayers the strengthening comfort needed on that last long journey.

The other little traits in his character told by his biographers fill in the picture. We learn how he always refused stole-fees,[137] how as Archbishop he began to preach in each church in turn till he had provoked the parish priests to take up sermons seriously themselves and deliver them well,[138] how when tired he would read his Breviary, saying daily, besides the prescribed portions, the seven Penitential Psalms, the Office of Our Lady, and, twice a week, the whole office of the dead. It was again his phenomenal memory coming to his help, for all the psalms he said by heart. He found it a rest to recite his Office, and thus by the repetition of familiar words to disengage his mind from the cares of his high charge and gradually push his consciousness down deeper and deeper into the endless depths of God, or make it climb higher and higher along the peaks of thought till all the inrushes of life and movement failed, and he found himself amidst the topmost summits of being, in the stillness and the silence, where no distraction is

---

[136] Ibid., 323.
[137] Ibid., 322.
[138] Ibid.

but God only. This is the character portrayed by his biographers, showing clearly in the authentic paintings of him. We see the shrewd, humorous mouth, the forceful lips, the straight determined nose, the gentle eyes looking out beyond this beautiful landscape of tangible creation to the ideal and uttermost beauty towards which his whole life marched. No doubt he had his failings of act and character. But they are difficult to discern in the blaze of all his greatness. Perhaps his unemotional temperament made him at times unsympathetic, perhaps his love of accuracy made him impatient of others' incompleteness, perhaps even his humour jarred at times on a sad and listless world.

But no echo of discord sounds through the ages. He appears only as a great "arm-fellow of God," in whose soul the Divine Beauty finds Narcissus-like the reflexion of Itself, whose life and character open Heaven's gates to Earth, and stand a

Swinging-wicket, set
Between
The Unseen and the Seen.[139]

---

[139] Francis Thompson, "Any Saint," in *The Works of Francis Thompson*, vol. 2, *Poems* (New York: Charles Scribner's Sons, 1913), 47.

X

Death and After

WITH all his multiplied labours, S. Antonino had strained to breaking point the bond between soul and body. The golden bowl, worn so fine, was breaking; the silver cord, stretched against such resistance, was fast loosening. The restless, wandering, wavering stranger, that had dwelt so long in its fleshly hostel, was anxious to be gone and find its rest at last in the house of its eternity. "But man," says the Saint, "whose memory is good and who has realized his life's brief span, grows thereby more full of energy as his years heap up."[140]

At the end of April, 1459, he caught a lingering fever which the physicians of that date called phlegmatic,[141] apparently tuberculosis or some inflammatory disease of the upper air-passages. He had always been threatened with consumption,[142] and this added to his weakened condition and his old age brought him very low. "Three score and ten," he murmured, "are the years of man."[143] He had passed his seventieth birthday.

On May 1st, the feast of SS. Philip and James, just before twilight surrounded by the friars of S.

---

[140] Antonino, *Summa Theologica Moralis*, I. 2, 4, i., 108.
[141] Société des Bollandistes, *Acta Sanctorum*, 326.
[142] Ibid., 319.
[143] Ibid., 327.

Marco, he received Extreme Unction. When the administration of the Sacrament was over, the brethren began to recite Matins. As they commenced Lauds, he intoned the *Deus in adjutorium*, "O God come to my assistance," with great devotion. After that came for the most part only broken phrases, for consciousness was slowly ebbing. The old memory however lingered, and the listening, anxious throng in his bedchamber caught the familiar sayings which had never been long absent from his lips: "To serve God is to reign"; and that cry to his mother: "Holy and unsullied Maidenhood, how fitly to praise thee, I know not." The tremulous voice was heard from time to time joining in the Divine Office, then, definitely and clearly, reciting the last Psalm of Lauds, always his favourite: "Praise ye the Lord in His Holy places. Praise ye Him in the firmament of His Power" (Ps. 150). As this ended, the Psalter was begun.

He lay silent—they thought unconscious. But in the 24th Psalm, he broke in and took up the verse "Towards the Lord are my eyes alway, for my feet shall He pluck from the snare." These words of patience and hope, of contrition, faith and love were the last that crossed his lips. Early next morning, May 2nd, the Eve of the Ascension, in kissing the figure of the Crucified, the old man died.

A touching proof of where lay the saintly Archbishop's heart was shown when his will was disclosed. He left his body to the friars of S. Marco and all the moneys to be found in his

palace to be distributed to the poor. After a pro-
longed search, only four ducats were discovered,
so faithful had he been to the spirit of his Master.
But despite this scanty legacy, right along the
route that led from the Duomo to S. Marco,
down the little street in which he had been born,
crowded the thronging people of Florence. For
the last time they saw their holy pastor go by,
carried to his resting-place by the hands of six
Bishops. In the pelting rain of that May morning, the huddled poor knelt, sobbing and praying, now for him, now to him. It was a wondrous
sight, for Pope Pius II, the brilliant, learned, err-
ing Pontiff of the Renaissance who happened to
be in the city, followed in the sad cortège. His
presence showed how, apart as the two had been
in temperament, pursuits, and sympathies, they
had yet worked together for the reform and
uplifting of the Church. The Cardinal of Venice,
a nephew of Eugenius IV, one of the Saint's
best friends, celebrated the Requiem Mass and
blessed the narrow grave. Over the sacred remains
was placed a heavy stone. A far more crushing
load saddened the hearts of the Florentine poor,
for he, their defender, their patron, their father,
whose time and counsel and strength had been
utterly spent for them, was no more to walk
among them. Miracles had he wrought unnum-
bered; miracles too were his very bones to work,
and the long unending tale of them can be read
in the Process of Canonization. The tomb at once
became a shrine. Waxen and wooden images of

healed and restored limbs became so numerous that they had to be perpetually removed to make room for others. It was only when the violent sack of the monastic buildings which preceded the murder of another great Dominican Prior of S. Marco, Girolamo Savonarola, had polluted the Church and preparations were being made for cleaning it out thoroughly, that all these ex-voto offerings were completely swept away.[144]

Into the story, necessarily monotonous, of these supernatural doings, we shall not enter. They are the same and must be the same in the history of every Saint. And after all, as said Fr. Santez, O.P., a well-loved disciple of the Archbishop, "Why recount his miracles? None of them, nor all of them, were ever so marvellous as his own blessed character." Indeed it is his character itself that wrought one astonishing work, which for its charm, its comfort, and its note of hopefulness shall here be set down.

When Prior of S. Marco, S. Antonino had received to the Dominican habit a certain Piedmontese, to whom he gave his own name of Antony. This young man as a priest was captured by pirates and carried off to Tunis. A certain vanity that this friar had about his preaching had always been a matter of anxiety to the Saint, but probably even he had not suspected how empty of God the priest's soul had become. After a brief imprisonment, he apostatised to

---

[144] Société des Bollandistes, *Acta Sanctorum*, 354.

Mahomedanism and broke through his priestly vows. When some months had been spent in sin, he heard of S. Antonino's death. Rumour, through some Genoese merchants, brought stories of the Saint's kindness and gentleness; and all the old world came back again to the hapless man's remembrance. He thought of his high ideals, nurtured by the calm wisdom of his Prior, then of his fall and sullied innocence. Moved to sorrow by the terrible contrast, he repented of his sin, publicly recanted his apostasy, and atoned for his wasted life by a martyr's death. Under the name of Bl. Antony Neyrot he is honoured now as a saint by his Dominican brethren (having been beatified by Pope Clement XIII), and his feast is kept on April 10th.

One other miracle must be told which calls back another of the Saint's own brethren. Two old ladies of Naples relate in the Process of Canonization how, when S. Antonino left Naples after his Priorship there, he gave them "a tiny sculptured figure of Death and a small painting by the hand of a certain devout friar, John the Artist, to which they had recourse, in temptation to the Death, in trouble to the painting. And as often as they thus prayed, in temptation and in trouble alike, they felt God's help.[145] The interest in this story lies in the identification of Friar John the Artist. No life of him mentions this miracle, no historian of him seems to have noticed

---

[145] Ibid., 347.

this painting, yet to whom else can it refer than Giovanni di Vecchio, artist, saint, and friend of S. Antonino, whom all the world reveres as Fra Angelico? Surely too it is fitting that the work of one, whose whole spirit was alive with childlike joy and peace, should bring to anxious, troubled hearts the rest and comfort of God.

It was under a Medici Pope, Leo X, that the testimony of witnesses for the Archbishop's heroic sanctity began to be taken. Under the succeeding Pontiff, Adrian VI, it was completed; and S. Antonino was solemnly enrolled in the Calendar of the Saints (May 31st, 1522). But it was not till the next year (November 26th, 1523), as Adrian died after a reign of only a few months, that the Bull of Canonization was promulgated by Clement VII, curiously enough another Medici.

The last notice of our Saint comes in the year 1589. A new and more worthy shrine had been prepared in a chapel of S. Marco, reared by the generosity of two brothers of the noble house of the Salviati. To this the sacred body was to be translated. After diligently learning from the older friars where, according to tradition, lay the relics of the Archbishop, Cardinal Alessandro de' Medici (later Pope Leo XI) began at night-fall, May 7th, 1589, the identifying of the body. In the presence of the Salviati, the Provincial of Tuscany, the Prior and many of the friars, he had the coffin lifted out and placed where all might see it. Then reverently the lid was taken off and all gazed on the form that had lain undisturbed for one hundred and thirty years. The face was perfectly recognisable. He was clothed simply in the Dominican habit, with no emblem of the episcopate, save for the pallium that marked out his jurisdiction as received from the See of Rome. The habit was slightly soiled. The limbs were intact, though, except for the face which was almost perfect, the bones and muscles were seemingly but barely covered by the tightly stretched skin. Even the number of the teeth is set down in the detailed description left by the Notary Public.

The next day, May 8th, took place the translation of the relics to the new shrine. Besides Cardinal Alessandro were four others of Rome's Princes, two Archbishops, seventeen Bishops, and an escort of reigning Italian sovereigns. Thus was the humble Archbishop brought in pomp to the place where all that is mortal of him rests to this day. It is only matter for regret that, fired no doubt with devotion and caught with the Renaissance spirit of splendour and display, they placed over his Dominican habit the full regalia of an Archbishop. A precious mitre encircled his brow, a glittering ring shone on his finger, a jewelled cross hung on his breast, a gorgeous cope compassed him about. How little could those devoted men have read the secret wishes of that cold, dead heart! How vain would all this have appeared to the Saint himself! How utterly at cross-purposes with his life, his character, his ideals!

There is another shrine which the devout lover of S. Antonino finds perhaps more appropriate and more touching—his cell in S. Marco. Here within these walls, how much of that character was built up which has made him revered in Florence, as the most blessed of her Bishops for over a thousand years! We look round with affection and love to think how much it meant, when in those far-off days (which somehow here seem not quite so distant) the vigorous Prior wrought out so many plans for the well-being of his brethren and the city. In it are gathered now his vestments, the death-mask, some manuscripts (which it requires a persistent visitor to get hold of) in his execrable handwriting, and an old portrait. One looks instinctively for the mark that the tilted chair dug into the wall.

But in this "narrow cell" that S. Antonino had chosen for himself, Fra Angelico has painted a fresco. Its design was no doubt thought out by the friends in counsel; and the Prior must have stood and watched while the artist-friar in prayer worked out with his bright colouring the mystery that both deemed the most appropriate. It represents the descent of Christ to the departed in Limbo. The figure of the Crucified Saviour, who has not yet burst through the portals of the tomb, stands in soft mellow light at the entrance of a rocky cave. In front and to the right stretch the long line of figures whose eyes gaze in rapt ineffable adoration on the face that lit up for them the gloom alike of life and of death. Thronging together, their hands uplifted in wonder, their knees half-bowed in worship, they stand for thousands and tens of thousands out of many nations and centuries and beliefs. Gathered from Earth's wide-stretching garden, they are the first blossoms that Christ shall offer to His Father; and over them all broods a hushed, yet living, silence. They are the spirits of the just made perfect, the first-fruits of the Lamb, the eldest-born of all the Dead. How they had waited in patience shut up within their prison, while through timeless æons they looked out for the Messias! Tired were they and weary, expectant of release, yet knowing not day nor hour when the fulness of time should come. In silence and in hope was their only and utter strength. So Christ would have them remain until He should come.

And S. Antonino, looking on this as he worked and laboured and wrote, learnt the lesson of life as taught by his friend Fra Angelico. Here, brimful of meaning, which yet would never tire or make afraid, was a splendid sermon by the most eloquent of Friar Preachers.

He looked and learned that patience in weariness, patience in waiting, patience in an incomplete state of being is the most precious virtue to have attained, so that "through patience we might have hope."

Bibliography

Alighieri, Dante. *Purgatorio*. In *The Divine Comedy*. Translated by Henry Wadsworth Longfellow. Leipzig: Berhard Tauchnitz, 1867.

Antonino. *Historia vel Chronicon*. 3 vols. Lyons: N.p., 1543.

Antonino. *Lettere di S. Antonino*. Firenze: Tipografia Berbèra, Bianchi e C., 1859.

Antonino. *Summa Theologica Moralis*. 4 vols. Verona: P. and B. Ballerini, 1740.

Bisticci, Vespasiano da. *Vite di Uomini Illustri del Secolo XV*. Firenze: Barbèra, Bianchi e comp., 1859.

Brocchi, Giuseppe Maria. *Vite de' Santi e Beati Fiorentini*. Firenze: La Stemperia di Gaetano Albizzini, 1742.

Creighton, Mandell. *A History of the Papacy During the Period of the Reformation*. Vol. 2. London: Longmans, Green & Co., 1882.

Domenicani, *Bullarium Ordinis Praedicatorum*. Vol. 4. Rome: Ex Typographia Hieronymi Mainardi, 1732.

Dominici, Giovanni. *Locula Noctis*. Edited by Remi Coulon. Paris: A. Picard, 1908.

Douglas, Robert Langton. *Fra Angelico*. London: G. Bell and Sons, 1902.

Échard, Jacques. *Scriptores Ordinis Praedicatorum Recensiti*. Vol. 1. Paris: Ballard et Simart, 1719.

Ferretti, Ludovico. *La Chiesa et il Convento di San Domenico di Fiesole*. Firenze: Tipografia di San Giuseppe, 1901.

Gardner, Edmund G. *The Story of Florence*. London: J. M. Dent & Co., 1903.

Godkin, G. S. *The Monastery of S. Marco*. London: J. M. Dent & Co., 1901.

Ilgner, Carl. *Die Volkswirtschaftlichen Anschauungen Antonius von Florenz*. Paderborn: Druck und Verlag von Ferdinand Schöningh, 1904.

Lecky, W. H. *History of the Rise and Influence of the Spirit of Rationalism in Europe*. Vol. 1. London: Longmans, Green & Co., 1910.

Loddi, F. Serafino Maria. *Memorie della Genalogia, del Luogo e del Nascimento di S. Antonino*. Firenze: N.p., 1731.

Loddi, F. Serafino Maria. *Riposta a un Amico in Ordine della Genealogia di S. Antonino*. Firenze: N.p., 1744.

Maccarani, Domenico. *Vita di S. Antonino Arcivenscovo di Firenze dell' Ordine de Predicatori*. Firenze: Stamperia di S.A.R., 1708.

Moro, Giovanni. *Di S. Antonino in Relazione alla Riforma Cattolica nel Secolo XV*. Firenze: B. Seeber, 1899.

Mortier, Daniel-Antonin. *Histoire des Maîtres Généraux de l'Ordre des Frères Prêcheurs*. 7 vols. Paris: Alphonse Picard et Fils, 1909.

Razzi, Girolamo. *Vita Miracoli. e Traslazione di S. Antonino Arcivescovo di Firenze*. N.p.: 1589.

Rösler, Augustin. *Kardinal Johannes Dominicis Erziehungslehre; und die übrigen pädagogischen Leistungen Italiens im 15. Jahrhundert*. Freiburg im Briesgau: Herdersche Verlagsbuchhandlug, 1894.

Scudder, Vida D., ed., trans. *Saint Catherine of Siena as Seen in Her Letters*. London: J. M. Dent & Sons, LTD., 1911.

Société des Bollandistes, *Acta Sanctorum*. Vol. 22, *Iunii, Tomus 2*. Paris: Société des Bollandistes, 1886.

Société des Bollandistes. *Acta Sanctorum*. Vol. 14, *Maii, Tomus 1*. Paris: Société des Bollandistes, 1886.

Thompson, Francis. "Any Saint." In *The Works of Francis Thompson*, vol. 2, *Poems*. New York: Charles Scribner's Sons, 1913.

Touron, Antoine. *Histoire des Hommes Illustres de l'Ordre de Saint Dominique*. Vol. 3. Paris: Babuty et Quillau, 1746.

Vasari, Giorgio. *Stories of Italian Artists*. Translated by E. L. Seeley. London: Chatto & Windus, 1906.

Venturi, Pietro Tacchi. *Storia della Compagna di Gesù in Italia*. Vol. 1. Roma-Milano: Società Editrice Dante Alighieri, 1910.

"X Mai: Saint Antonin, Archevêque de Florence." In *Année Dominicaine: ou vies des saints, des bienheureux, des martyrs, et des autres personnes illustres ou recommandables par leur piété de l'un et de l'autre sexe de l'Ordre des Frères-Prêcheurs, distribuées suivant les jours de l'année.*, edited by The Dominican Order of Preachers, 279–305. Lyons: X. Jevain, 1891.

N.B.—By the courtesy of the Rev. Michael Browne, O.P., the author has been allowed the use of valuable manuscript notes left by the late Rev. Charles Priest, O.P., at S. Peter's Priory, Hinckley, which have been most helpful in writing chapters II and III.

XIII Books is dedicated to publishing new and vintage works centered around politics, the economy, and the family. Named after Pope Leo XIII—the pope of the "working man," whose pontificate was the first to comprehensively engage in the Church's relationship with the modern world—our imprint was born out of the conviction that we cannot separate the Catholic faith from our involvement with the world around us, and that the social doctrine of the Church, whether explicitly or implicitly, requires a commitment by Catholics to transform every aspect of the social order in conformity to the will of God. We aspire to earn a reputation amongst our readers as a reliable provider of the best the social tradition has to offer, which is rooted in our allegiance to Christ the King and passion for sharing with others the teachings of the Church.